GEORGE CLOONEY

Recent Titles in Greenwood Biographies

J.R.R. Tolkien: A Biography
Leslie Ellen Jones

Colin Powell: A Biography
Richard Steins

Pope John Paul II: A Biography
Meg Greene Malvasi

Al Capone: A Biography
Luciano Iorizzo

George S. Patton: A Biography
David A. Smith

Gloria Steinem: A Biography
Patricia Cronin Marcello

Billy Graham: A Biography
Roger Bruns

Emily Dickinson: A Biography
Connie Ann Kirk

Langston Hughes: A Biography
Laurie F. Leach

Fidel Castro: A Biography
Thomas M. Leonard

Oprah Winfrey: A Biography
Helen S. Garson

Mark Twain: A Biography
Connie Ann Kirk

Jack Kerouac: A Biography
Michael J. Dittman

Mother Teresa: A Biography
Meg Greene

GEORGE CLOONEY

A Biography

Joni Hirsch Blackman

GREENWOOD BIOGRAPHIES

GREENWOOD PRESS
An Imprint of ABC-CLIO, LLC

A B C 🔅 C L I O

Santa Barbara, California • Denver, Colorado • Oxford, England

Library of Congress Cataloging-in-Publication Data

Blackman, Joni Hirsch.
  George Clooney : a biography / Joni Hirsch Blackman.
    p. cm. — (Greenwood biographies)
  Includes bibliographical references and index.
    ISBN 978-0-313-35826-5 (hardcover : alk. paper) — ISBN 978-0-313-35827-2 (ebook) 1. Clooney, George. 2. Actors—United States—Biography. I. Title. II. Series.
  PN2287.C546B43   2010
  791.4302'8092—dc22   2009034910
  [B]

14 13 12 11 10   1 2 3 4 5

This book is also available on the World Wide Web as an eBook.
Visit www.abc-clio.com for details.

ABC-CLIO, LLC
130 Cremona Drive, P.O. Box 1911
Santa Barbara, California 93116-1911

This book is printed on acid-free paper ∞

Manufactured in the United States of America

For my mom, Helen Hammes Hirsch,
who always wanted me to be Barbara Walters.

CONTENTS

Series Foreword   ix

Introduction   xi

Timeline: Events in the Life of George Clooney   xxiii

Chapter 1   Cute, Right from the Beginning   1

Chapter 2   Everyone's Famous   13

Chapter 3   The Acting Bug   31

Chapter 4   Pilots, Movies, and *Sisters*   43

Chapter 5   *ER*—The Right Thing   57

Chapter 6   A Movie Star   69

Chapter 7   Goodbye, *ER*; Hello, Beautiful People   85

Chapter 8   George versus the Stalkerazzi   97

Chapter 9   History Student   105

Chapter 10 Good Luck   115

Chapter 11 "Academy Award Winner George Clooney"   123

CONTENTS

Chapter 12   Messenger of Peace   129
Chapter 13   Becoming Paul Newman   141

Selected Bibliography   155
Index   157

Photo essay follows page 96

SERIES FOREWORD

In response to high school and public library needs, Greenwood developed this distinguished series of full-length biographies specifically for student use. Prepared by field experts and professionals, these engaging biographies are tailored for high school students who need challenging yet accessible biographies. Ideal for secondary school assignments, the length, format and subject areas are designed to meet educators' requirements and students' interests.

Greenwood offers an extensive selection of biographies spanning all curriculum-related subject areas including social studies, the sciences, literature and the arts, history and politics, as well as popular culture, covering public figures and famous personalities from all time periods and backgrounds, both historic and contemporary, who have made an impact on American and/or world culture. Greenwood biographies were chosen based on comprehensive feedback from librarians and educators. Consideration was given to both curriculum relevance and inherent interest. The result is an intriguing mix of the well known and the unexpected, the saints and sinners from long-ago history and contemporary pop culture. Readers will find a wide array of subject choices from fascinating crime figures like Al Capone to inspiring pioneers like Margaret Mead, from the greatest minds of our time like Stephen Hawking to the most amazing success stories of our day like J. K. Rowling.

While the emphasis is on fact, not glorification, the books are meant to be fun to read. Each volume provides in-depth information about the subject's life from birth through childhood, the teen years, and adulthood. A thorough account relates family background and education, traces personal and professional influences, and explores struggles, accomplishments, and contributions. A timeline highlights the most significant life events against a historical perspective. Bibliographies supplement the reference value of each volume.

INTRODUCTION

The spectrum of awards bestowed upon George Clooney runs from an Oscar (for Best Supporting Actor for his role in *Syriana*) to the title "Sexiest Man Alive" (awarded—twice—by *People* magazine) to a place on *Time* magazine's list of the "100 Most Influential People" (three times).[1] He was also named one of *People*'s "Most Beautiful People" in 2000, came in at number one on *People*'s list of the most eligible bachelors, also in 2000, was given a spot on *Vanity Fair*'s list of the best-dressed men, and was chosen as the "celebrity all women want to date."

Then again, he was named "the most kissable man in Hollywood" by a Harlequin Enterprises survey, and Wrigley found him the man "most people would like to share a piece of gum with."[2]

From one of those awards came this spot-on description: "Those sensuous lips, those curfew-breaking eyes, the head-down forgot-my-homework mug that makes you want to either mother him or smother him with kisses? To most men it doesn't ring a bell, but many women recognize in *ER*'s George Clooney everything they loved in their first boyfriend."[3]

Not just handsome, the top-notch actor has been called "The Last Movie Star" by *Time*. He is also a respected writer and director over whom women swoon and with whom guys want to hang out on the basketball court. *Newsweek*'s John Horn called him "a happily married woman's just-once fantasy."[4]

But few who really know him would use any of those various titles to describe him. The one word, without contest, most people use to describe this mega-movie star?

Nice.

Though he's obviously talented and has an impeccable sense of style and undeniable charisma, he invariably, and with his famous self-deprecation, claims he has just been lucky.

No surprise there, really—his father has said the same thing about his own successful career. Asked once by an elementary school teacher how he got through tough times in his broadcasting and news career when he was criticized or rejected, Nick Clooney wrote, in his *Cincinnati Post* column: "There were many of those times, Dianna. I've been canceled and pilloried as much as anyone in our area, I suppose. I've also been inordinately praised." He added, "My formula is, I'm afraid, luck. The luck of a loving family and friends who bolstered my confidence to accept adversity and get on with my life."[5]

A loving family and friends have also been key to George Clooney's success. But George consistently also gives a solid nod to his old man's benefactor—luck.

"Sometimes you get too much credit for things," Clooney said.[6] "If one of those crappy pilots had been picked up, I wouldn't have been available to do *ER*. And if *ER* had been put on Friday night instead of Thursday night, I don't have a film career. It's luck."

"I'm very, very lucky that I was 33, 34 before the show [*ER*] hit," Clooney said another time.[7] "I'd done eight series before that. But, you know, I was making money, so sometimes I get too much credit. People say, 'Oh, you struggled.' But I was making regular series money for 10 years, so I wasn't struggling; I was beating the odds. I owned a house, I never had to worry about money, I could always afford a car and an apartment. . . . So I was very lucky. I wasn't doing great work, and I wasn't very good at it, but I was beating the odds. And I'm very lucky I didn't get famous at those points, because it would have ruined any chance of me being here today."

Nick Clooney could arguably named be the "most influential person" in George Clooney's life. In fact, George once told a newspaper he and his father are "twins in many ways—including being stubborn and having a temper."[8] *Entertainment Weekly*, after a lengthy interview with Clooney, concluded, "Despite all of his wealth and fame—or maybe because of it—Clooney still measures himself against his father."[9]

Regardless of how he got to be who he is, the man is embraced by nearly all he meets. Over and over and over, people interviewed, from Hollywood to Kentucky to Washington, D.C., who have spent time with Clooney for an hour or a day or much longer or who knew George throughout vastly different times in his life describe exactly the same person: funny, charming, a goofy practical joker who is witty, generous, self-deprecating and, always, nice.

"People like to ask me what are Hollywood stars like," TV critic John Kiesewetter of the *Cincinnati Enquirer*, who has covered Clooney since 1985, told me. "I can honestly say George Clooney is one of the nicest guys in the world. He's as nice as you'd want him to be."

Craig Kopp of the *Cincinnati Post*, another hometown journalist who covered Clooney, wrote in 1996—14 years after Clooney went to Hollywood and two years after his catapult to success on *ER*—"Clooney is apparently unaffected by his stardom. He doesn't wear the aura of an actor with a hit TV show or one who has starred opposite Ms. Pfeiffer and Nicole Kidman. How is Clooney managing to keep his ego in check?"[10]

Clooney answered the question: "Being 35 years old, as opposed to 25 years old, I think, is a big plus. Having thought you had a couple of big breaks and nothing happening and having been semi-successful several times and then not. And, having an aunt who was very successful and then not. You have a great understanding of this business, which has very little to do with you."

Even years and many high-profile movies later, Clooney's father proudly wrote in his column that his son was unaffected by his skyrocketing fame.

"What we can tell all of his friends is that the pressure—the really unimaginable pressure—of a high profile career has not changed George. He has matured and grown in many ways, but he remains firmly grounded in common sense and good humor."[11]

Such humility is his family's legacy, perhaps one of the reasons the superstar prefers such things as riding in nondescript SUVs to stretch limousines. He doesn't show up with an entourage in most cases and returns phone calls to his publicist himself, often leaving his home phone number with reporters.

The mayor of Maysville, where Nick and his sister, singer Rosemary Clooney, grew up, commented in 2003 about Nick Clooney's candidacy for Congress: "The Clooneys are the Kentucky Kennedys," said David Cartmell. "Nick's been all over the country, but like the rest of his family, he's never forgotten where he came from."[12]

George's old friends say exactly same thing about a man who well remembers his friends from the places he grew up—Mason, Ohio; Augusta and Maysville, Kentucky; and Cincinnati.

Mary Ellen Tanner, a singer who performed on Nick Clooney's variety show in the early 1970s, when George was a child, got to know young George when he hung around his father's studio. About 30 years later, at a celebration of Nick's 50 years in broadcasting, she entered the room to perform, and George spotted her.

"George yelled out, 'Hey, Mary Ellen!' and came over and hugged me and said, 'I grew up with you!'" said Tanner in an interview. "He's obviously an international superstar, but when I see him, he's the same."

George's loyalty to old friends is legendary, particularly regarding the close group of friends known as "The Boys" with whom he hangs out on a regular basis. The group consists of guys he met when he first arrived in Hollywood. Those same friends have stuck by him when the lean years fattened up.

At the premiere of Clooney's blockbuster film *Batman & Robin*, in 1997, the row marked "George Clooney" in the theater was filled, his father said, "not with big names or big executives to match his big career. It was filled with friends from the lean days and with family. George would be surprised that anyone thought that remarkable. Which is the real reason his mother and I were proud of our son Thursday night."[13]

Clooney's loyalty to his friends is, indeed, legendary. Clooney friend Bonnie Hunt said, "He's the guy who takes care of everything, leads the pack and includes all the guys in his success. Success would be horrible for him without his friends around."[14]

Stories about Clooney and his various buddies when they were younger abound around Hollywood. Many of his pals would bunk in his home when they needed a place to plop—much as he did to some of them when he arrived there with little cash and a beat-up car. As the jobs got better, The Boys' activities went more upscale—such as a cross-country golf vacation on a rock 'n' roll tour bus.

"Because I don't take too many vacations and I've been, essentially, working 14 years straight—now, I'm not complaining. I cut tobacco in Kentucky and that's a lot worse and a lot less pay," said Clooney.[15] "But there are times when I have a weekend off and I'll call up the boys and say, 'We're all going to Boise for the weekend to go whitewater rafting.' And you charter a jet and you stick your eight best friends on the plane."

"We've all been together for 15 years," he said.[16] "It's a big web of fun. Sundays, everybody comes by and everybody plays basketball, and we're all really close and really supportive of one another."

"We are what makes him George," says actor Richard Kind, one of The Boys, who met Clooney when they played brothers on a pilot. "Everything else makes him George Clooney. Things are very difficult with The Boys right now. One [Clooney] is a superstar. He has shot to the heights. Others are in various stages of career. We have to work hard to maintain the communication. George is the hub. He's the one who initiates it."[17]

For some celebrities, when their press regarding anything becomes "legendary," the same stories continue to circulate as the truth becomes lost in the passage of time. With Clooney, however, the idea that his reputation has outlived its accuracy is doubtful. A United Nations peacekeeping official who traveled to Africa for three weeks with Clooney in 2008—yes, he's a philanthropist, too (one of his odder philanthropic gestures came in 2007, when he sold a kiss for $350,000 at a charity auction in the south of France)—repeated the mantra.

"Not only is he the nicest guy, he's as smart as anyone, he's normal, he's interested, he's engaged, he's fun to toss a baseball with, he's just a terrific guy. It's terrible, all the hype is true," Nick Birnback told me with a laugh in an interview.

He then grew more serious. "It's inspiring. You can't work for the U.N. without getting some cynicism, but it was inspiring meeting someone who really has gotten the royal flush in life and manages to retain a sense of self and humility, without false modesty. He's incredibly generous with his time, with his friends, to the people around him. He manages 'IT' as well as anyone I've ever seen. And what he adds on top of it is a remarkably acute political intelligence. He can go right to the heart of the matter on key issues as well as most trained political analysts. Behind the grin and the chin, he's deceptively sharp and improbably well-informed. . . He's a guy who's very grounded, who is tight with his folks, whose friends are buddies he's hung out with for decades—that's the thing that gives him the ability to live with the larger craziness and nuttiness. He's very rooted."

A glowing tribute, to be sure. But the man is most definitely not a boring saint. His love of a good time is well documented, and some say he can be difficult—usually when he is sticking his neck out to speak up for someone or something. This is also, after all, a man who, at least at one point, had his own remote-controlled whoopee cushion.[18]

"In pursuit of a punch line, Clooney has been known to shove all manner of props up his nose, turn a Super Soaker on fellow cast members and replace the hard-boiled eggs on a catering table with raw ones," said *People*.[19]

One of his famous pranks was more long term. He told his pal Kind that he was taking an art class and later gave him a painting of a nude woman that he actually found in a trash can. The artwork hung in Kind's home for quite a while before Clooney admitted what he'd done.

Augusta natives all have their own favorite prank from George's childhood including once during a high school science project when he made a roomful of girls scream by letting loose the mice used in his experiment. Though he's grown up, he has never lost that boyish enthusiasm.

"He's a modern-day Clark Gable, with the mischievousness of a 10-year-old boy," wrote Cindy Pearlman of the *Chicago Sun-Times*.[20] *ER* co-star Juliana Margulies put it this way: "George is a grown-up with a kid's heart."[21]

This is the guy who spent $1,500 renting flowers and tables to trick tabloid reporters into thinking Brad Pitt and Angelina Jolie were going to get married at his Italian villa. The antics on the set of the *Ocean's 11* set were constant—such as when Clooney put a coat of Vaseline on every doorknob of producer Jerry Weintraub's suite at the Bellagio hotel, causing Weintraub to yell "Where the hell is Clooney?" During the filming of that movie, Weintraub said, "The pranks here are akin to *Animal House*."[22]

Clooney can pull pranks in groups and on his own, and no event is exempt. He made sure he increased the size of his legacy when he stepped foot, literally, in famous Hollywood cement.

Before the big event at Grauman's Chinese Theater, in 2007, Clooney's father noticed his son's familiar mischievous look. His parents asked what he was up to. He reminded them of the time he'd visited California as a child, looked at all of the famous handprints and footprints in front of the theater, and shook his head over how small their hands and feet had been. Maybe the concrete had shrunk the prints when it dried, Nick Clooney suggested to his son.

George figured he'd take things into his own hands. Knowing he'd been asked to donate the shoes he wore for the prints to the museum across the street, he bought a special pair for the occasion. Though the star wears a size 11, he got a size 14 that day.

"If some kid comes along in 20 or 30 years, he probably won't remember who George Clooney was, but he won't be able to miss the footprints," Clooney said.[23]

Though everyday he walks in some very big footprints—those of his Aunt Rosemary, his Uncle George, and his father, Nick—George Clooney has famously suggested he won't be having any offspring walking in his. He told Barbara Walters[24] he will never remarry (after a short marriage in 1989 to Talia Balsam) and has not only declared but made two bets that he isn't cut out to be a dad (though friends say he is one incredible uncle to his sister's two children).

On the other end of the spectrum, he also charms those older than he is—from the time he worked at a department store selling shoes as a college student, when coworkers said he was very popular with the older women, to a news item from 2004 that praised Clooney's gallantry after he carried a grandmother's groceries uphill near his villa in Italy.[25]

Clint Eastwood said Clooney's constant movie theme is "doing the right thing, as opposed to the expedient thing." True in his life, as well as his work.[26]

That's certainly true when it comes to standing up for people and causes he believes in. He has spoken up for colleagues he felt were being treated unfairly and has led several protests against overzealous paparazzi.

In its story naming Clooney the "Sexiest Man Alive," in 1997, *People* said, "To many, his willingness to take a stand no matter the consequences was just a measure of his character. 'That's one of his sexy qualities,' says *From Dusk till Dawn* costar Salma Hayek. 'He's incredibly brave.' Indeed, says Les Moonves, 'George is the guy who would quit the most important opportunity of his life if he felt it threatened his integrity.' "[27]

Director Steven Soderbergh, who has worked with Clooney on several movies, agreed: "George has a very strong moral code about the right way to behave and the wrong way to behave. A lot of people who are famous don't have that code."[28]

Batman director Joel Schumacher concludes, "George gives me faith that there are still some really terrific people that success comes to who handle it beautifully."[29]

When asked to describe the George Clooney she knew before his incredible success, his *Sisters* series costar Heather McAdam told me in an interview, "The first thing that comes to mind is he's a class act, through and through. Women love him and men want to be him. He's very professional and how do you throw in . . . he's funny! He was always making everybody laugh. I think sometimes he bent over backward to make everybody laugh. He's a very funny person. He's just adorable."

McAdam worked with Clooney from 1993 to 1994. "I'd say he was approachable, he treated everybody the same, from the crew to celebrities. He had the likeability factor—there's a humanness to him. He approaches things happening in our world in a way that he feels connected to people—there are no airs about him. I could tell he was politically aware even back then."

One of the "boys," a former fellow struggling actor he met in acting class, Grant Heslov, became his partner in Smoke House, their film and TV production company.

"He's a throwback to what movie stars used to be," Heslov says.[30] "You see him and you think, 'Wouldn't that be a great life?' He seems like a man's man. He seems like you could meet him at a bar and have a chat with him and it would be easy. And all of that is true."

Perhaps the best summary of George Clooney's life came from Rick Nicita, chairman of the American Cinematheque board, which honored Clooney in 2006 for his film achievements and offscreen social activism, calling him "truly a Renaissance man."[31]

"In a relatively short time, he has proven his talents as an actor, director, writer and producer," Nicita said. "He has managed to blend entertainment with political commentary as well as combining charm, eloquence and good old-fashioned movie star charisma."

Despite the consistent information about George Clooney and all that his friends, both those who knew him "when" and those he still sees often, say about him, it is of course possible that he is unlike his image. According to no less an expert than Clooney's own father, "nobody knows anybody."

Writing about biographies in general in his *Post* column in 1998, Nick Clooney complained that, although his job on the American Movie Channel required him to read many biographies, "biographies are superficial and filled with speculation," and most are "inaccurate and misleading," particularly when the subject himself declined to participate in the project.

"In a new book about a famous movie star, the author tells us she politely declined to cooperate. He wrote it anyway. He quoted people who claimed to be her best friends. We are not told if he talked to the 'friends' himself or simply cadged the quotes from other interviews. Some conclusions are based on remarks made by friends of the friend of the woman in question. A phone call with a person twice removed from the subject. Much of the rest simply came from newspaper accounts, fan magazines and gossip columns. The most scurrilous charges, none based on any evidence that would stand the test of law or history, are presented in declarative sentences."[32]

This volume, alas, also received a polite decline, not from the subject directly but from his publicist. It was written anyway, without the help of any "best" friends, because George Clooney's best friends, for their own reasons, wouldn't answer our phone calls without the publicist's OK. But it was written with the firsthand help of many people who have known George well over the years, as well as people who worked directly with him long ago and recently.

Newspaper accounts have been taken from respected publications, many from Clooney's "hometown" newspapers, the *Cincinnati Enquirer* and the now-defunct *Cincinnati Post*. Gossip columns and fan magazines were completely ignored.

Clooney's "melancholy conclusion" about biographies notwithstanding, I believe what follows is as true an account of George Clooney's life as can be written without his input.

Consider George Clooney's own father's answer, which appeared in his *Post* column, to a question about his son that was put to him in 1998 by a fourth grader: "What do you like best about George?" Clooney answered in a few short words, like a true old-school journalist: "That he's a nice guy."[33]

As *Michael Clayton* costar Tom Wilkinson put it a decade later, "It would be nice if prodigiously gifted, handsome, multi-millionaire George Clooney were in fact a bastard. He isn't."[34]

Joel Stein, who spent two evenings interviewing George Clooney, concluded, "I feel as if I failed. In seven hours, I wasn't able to find a part of Clooney different from the one everyone already knows."[35]

In many, many more hours of reading and conducting interviews, that's my conclusion, as well.

NOTES

1. *Time*, "100 Most Influential People" for 2007 (May 14, 2007, p. 81), 2008 (May 12, 2008, p. 108), and 2009 (May 11, 2009, p. 104). Clooney is listed under Heroes for 2007, under Arts Entertainment for 2008, and under Heroes and Icons for 2009.

2. "George Clooney: 50 Most Beautiful People of 2003," *People*, May 12, 2003, p. 90.

3. "George Clooney: 50 Most Beautiful People in the World 1996," *People*, May 6, 1996, p. 127.

4. John Horn, "George Clooney Rolls the Dice," *Newsweek*, December 17, 2001, p. 64.

5. Nick Clooney, "Students Keep Letters Coming," *Cincinnati Post*, May 20, 1998, p. 1C.

6. Chris Nashawaty, "The Last Great Movie Star," *Entertainment Weekly*, December 2, 2005, p. 44.

7. Jenelle Riley, "Charismatic Clooney Relies on More Than That," *Ventura County Star*, December 9, 2005, p. 4 (Life, Arts and Living).

8. John Kiesewetter, "George Clooney: Look Who's Talking Prime Time," *Cincinnati Enquirer*, July 25, 1990, p. B-1.

9. Nashawaty, "The Last Great Movie Star."

10. Craig Kopp, "Michelle Pfeiffer Talks About Being a Mother," *Cincinnati Post*, December 19, 1996, Perspective 12.

11. Nick Clooney, "George, Book Both Doing Well," *Cincinnati Post*, December 16, 2002, p. C1.

12. Cindy Schroeder, "Clooneys are KY's Kennedys," *Cincinnati Enquirer*, November 25, 2003, p. A1.

13. Nick Clooney, "Batman Makes Parents Proud," *Cincinnati Post*, June 16, 1997, p. 1B.

14. Cynthia Sanz, "Sexiest Man Alive 1997/George Clooney," *People*, November 17, 1997, p. 77.

15. Craig Kopp, "Gorgeous George's Life at the Top," *Cincinnati Post*, June 25, 1998, Perspective 16.

16. Lorrie Lynch, *USA Weekend*, September 26–28,1997, http://www.usa weekend.com/97_issues/970928/970928cov_clooney.html.

17. Ibid.

18. "50 Most Beautiful People in the World," *People*, May 8, 1995, p. 70.

19. Sanz, "Sexiest Man Alive 1997/George Clooney."

20. Cindy Pearlman, "Dr. Feelgood—Clooney Is Ready for Film Success," *Chicago Sun-Times*, June 21, 1998, Showcase 3.

21. Anne-Marie O'Neill, "Boy George—At 40, George Clooney Seems as Committed as Ever to His Buddies, Basketball, a Certain Potbellied Pig—And Bachelorhood," *People*, May 7, 2001, p. 96.

22. O'Neill, "Boy George."

23. Nick Clooney, "George's 'Bigfoot' Now Part of History," *Cincinnati Post*, June 20, 2007, p. C1.

24. *Barbara Walters Special*, ABC-TV, broadcast, November 17, 1995.

25. Frances D'Emilion, "Movie Star Clooney Strives to Be 'Bravo,'" *Cincinnati Post*, July 13, 2004.

26. *American Masters: You Must Remember This: The Warner Bros. Story*, September 25, 2008, PBS. Quoted in "The Clooney Factor" in the fifth and final hour, called "The Big Tent, 1980–Present."

27. Sanz, "The Sexiest Man Alive 1997/George Clooney."

28. Jamie Portman, "ER Star Dumps Little Screen for the Big One," *Southam Newspapers*, June 25, 1998, p. D9.

29. "George Clooney—Soaring as a Hollywood Superhero, He Comes Down Hard on Star Exploitation," *People*, December 30, 1996, p. 60.

30. Joel Stein, "Guess Who Came to Dinner?" *Time*, March 3, 2008, p. 46.

31. John Kiesewetter, "Clooney Honored for Films, Activism," *Cincinnati Enquirer*, June 8, 2006, p. 2A.

32. Nick Clooney, "Biographies Let Readers Down," *Cincinnati Post*, January 7, 1998, p. 1C.

33. Nick Clooney, "Students Keep Letters Coming."

34. Stein, "Guess Who Came to Dinner?"

35. Ibid.

TIMELINE: EVENTS IN THE LIFE OF GEORGE CLOONEY

May 6, 1961   George Timothy Clooney born in Lexington, Kentucky.

1967   Attends Blessed Sacrament School, Fort Mitchell, Kentucky and St. Michael's School, Columbus, Ohio.

1968   Attends Western Row Elementary School, Mason, Ohio.

1969   Attends St. Susanna School, Mason, Ohio.

1974   Moves to Augusta, Kentucky.

1979   Graduates from Augusta High School, enrolls in Northern Kentucky University.

1981   Gets a part as an extra in a film, *And They're Off*, shot in Lexington, Kentucky.

1982   Moves to Los Angeles.

1984   Gets part in a play, *Vicious*; first TV role on an episode of *Riptide*; plays Ace in *E/R*.

1985   Plays George Burnett in *Facts of Life* and Kevin Stark in *Street Hawk*.

1986   Plays Major Biff Woods in *Combat High*.

1987   Appears in two TV series, *Murder, She Wrote* and *The Golden Girls*; plays Oliver in *Return to Horror High*.

1988 Gets role as Roseanne's boss, Booker Brooks, on *Roseanne*; plays Matt Stevens in *Return of the Killer Tomatoes*.

1989 Plays Remar in *Red Surf*; marries Talia Balsam.

1990 Plays Chic Cesbro in *Sunset Beat* and Rick Stepjack in *Knights of the Kitchen Table*; "Uncle George" dies.

1991 Plays Joe in *Baby Talk*.

1992 Plays Detective Ryan Walker in *Bodies of Evidence*.

1993 Plays Detective James Falconer in *Sisters* and Bonnie's fiancé in *The Building*; divorces Talia Balsam.

1994 Takes role of Dr. Doug Ross in *ER*.

1995 Interviewed by Barbara Walters, says he will never marry again.

1996 Plays Seth Gecko in *From Dusk till Dawn* and Jack Taylor in *One Fine Day*, with Michelle Pfeiffer.

1997 Stars in *Batman & Robin*, stars in *The Peacemaker* with Nicole Kidman; named "Sexiest Man Alive" by *People*.

1998 Plays Jack Foley in *Out of Sight*, with Jennifer Lopez, and Captain Bosche in *The Thin Red Line*.

1999 Plays Archie Gates in *Three Kings*.

2000 Executive produces and stars as Colonel Jack Grady in *Fail-Safe*; stars as Everett in *O Brother Where Art Thou?*; stars in *The Perfect Storm*.

2001 Plays Danny Ocean in *Ocean's Eleven*; wins Golden Globe for *O Brother, Where Art Thou?*

2002 Produces, executive produces, and stars as Jerzy in *Welcome to Collinwood*; directs and stars as Jim Byrd in *Confessions of a Dangerous Mind*; stars in *Solaris*.

2003 Plays Miles in *Intolerable Cruelty*, with Catherine Zeta-Jones; executive produces *K Street*.

2004 Stars in *Ocean's Twelve*.

2005 Directs, writes. and stars as Fred Friendly in *Good Night, and Good Luck*; executive produces and stars as Bob Barnes in *Syriana*; executive produces and directs *Unscripted*.

2006   Wins Academy Award for Best Supporting Actor for *Syriana*; plays Jake Geismer in *The Good German*; named "Sexiest Man Alive" by *People* for second time; Max the pig dies on Dec. 1.

2007   Executive produces and stars as Michael Clayton in *Michael Clayton* and plays Danny Ocean in *Ocean's Thirteen*; narrates *Sand and Sorrow*, a documentary about Darfur; listed at number 13 on *Entertainment Weekly's* list of "The 50 Smartest People in Hollywood"; named to *Time's* list of the "100 Most Influential People in the World" (in the category Heroes and Pioneers).

2008   Nominated for the Academy Award as best actor for *Michael Clayton*; named to *Time's* list of the "100 Most Influential People in the World" (in the category Arts and Entertainment); plays Dodge Connelly in *Leatherheads* and Harry Pfarrer in *Burn after Reading*; breaks up with Sarah Larson in June.

2009   Returns to *ER* for one of the final episodes; plays Lyn Cassady in *The Men Who Stare at Goats*; plays Ryan Bingham in *Up in the Air*; is the voice of Mr. Fox in *The Fantastic Mr. Fox*.

Chapter 1

CUTE, RIGHT FROM
THE BEGINNING

Some people change quite a bit from the time they are children until they grow into adults; some do not. George Clooney, born on May 6, 1961, in Lexington, Kentucky, is apparently one of the latter.

When his friends and family remember George as a child, they use many of the same descriptions they use to describe him as an adult, more than 40 years later: he was a cute, funny, attention-seeker whose remarks were witty and amusing and whose quirky facial expressions were memorable.

His aunt, singer Rosemary Clooney, called young George a determined boy. "In a household with a lot of great kids around, he would get on a chair to get attention. He worked hard, he always had a way of getting around you, and he was cute. Cute, right from the beginning."[1]

And right from the beginning, Clooney remembers knowing that people were watching him. He didn't become famous on his own until he was in his 30s, but he felt the public's interest in his life long before that because his dad, Nick, was a popular disc jockey and TV news anchor in Cincinnati.[2] Not only did Nick Clooney bring his family along on his various personal appearances and even, sometimes, to work, but

George looked so much like his well-known dad that people made the obvious connection immediately even when they weren't together.

From the time he was a boy, Clooney also had an innate sense of fairness, something he would be known for later as an actor. As young as 18 months old, George stood up for people who were wronged—though, at this point, the person who was wronged was just himself. As he was playing with a litter of puppies at his grandmother's farm as a child, he was bitten by one of the puppies. "So he picked up the puppy by the tail and head and bit it back," his father said. "There's a certain justice there, so I couldn't get mad at him. 'You bite me, I'll bite you.' And he still does that, too."[3]

George remembered being asked as a child what he wanted to be when he grew up. "I want to be famous," he would answer. "I thought that was a job."[4] Perhaps he thought he'd be a drummer. His favorite possession as a kid was a snare drum he wore around his neck. "My parents hated it because I banged on it all day long. It had a removable top, so I could put things in it, put the top back on and keep playing," he said.[5] Just another way to make himself heard.

George's screen debut came on his dad's variety show when George was five, playing a leprechaun in a St. Patrick's Day special. Clooney's mom, Nina, often entertained the variety show audience while George worked the cue cards and did skits and commercials. The kid was so funny, his parents always thought George would become a stand-up comedian.[6]

His aunt Rosemary agreed: "He always had a smart answer and a kind of skewed look at the world. I thought he was going to be Don Rickles, he turned out to be Tyrone Power."[7]

Never underestimate the power of the cuteness factor—or the power of an upbringing. George's childhood was celebrity centered. His well-known dad made as many as 200 personal appearances a year at public functions around Cincinnati. Nick's family often went along and participated, which sometimes made for some interesting rides to and from various festivals and fairs. George, who friends say is "always on" when he has an audience, spent many childhood afternoons in tense car rides that would smooth into happy-face shows when the car arrived at its destination. Afterwards, the sulking was done in private.[8]

Nick's job necessitated multiple moves for the Clooneys while George and his year-older sister, Ada, were small. They attended various elementary schools—Blessed Sacrament School in Fort Mitchell, Kentucky; St. Michael's School in Columbus, Ohio; and the Western Row and St. Susanna schools in Mason, Ohio.

At Blessed Sacrament, where Joan Dressman taught Clooney to read in her first grade classroom, she once joked, "I had him three times a day for an hour each time. That's why he reads so well. I stressed expression!"[9]

At Western Row, George Clooney appeared in a second-grade Christmas production. "Dear Santa," he sang, "I just got the measles and I need your help right away—imagine me getting the measles and Christmas just two days away!"

Not quite Aunt Rosemary in *White Christmas*, but vocal music teacher Carol Rauch said George and Ada looked adorable wearing their pajamas, with red colored-pencil dots on their faces as they sang in front of the chorus in 1969. Rauch remembered the Clooneys as "the nicest family" and George as a cute little boy with "those piercing dark brown eyes."[10]

"I'm no dope. With their dad on TV, I figured they'd attract attention. I gave him his start, and he never came back and said, 'thanks,' or 'here's a residual,' nothing!" joked Rauch, who teaches at the University of Cincinnati. "I'm sure he doesn't remember it as fondly as I do. I hope it is what spurred him on!"[11]

It was about that time George was diagnosed with dyslexia, something his mother also had and that he, like his mother, grew out of later. Like most bright dyslexics, Nina Clooney said, he learned to compensate. "George got through school by charming his teachers," she said—another skill learned in childhood that Clooney held onto throughout his life.[12] When Clooney the adult is discussed, the word "charm" is always among the top 10 adjectives.

But in Mason, he didn't charm everyone, at least at first, said Anne Harpen, whose big brother Pete was an early friend of George's and who is still a friend. They met at St. Susanna, where Harpen remembered George as an active little boy with something unusual the other kids were jealous of—a famous father. That envy caused some of his classmates to pick on George.[13]

"In my family, we were always taught to be nice to everybody and he and my brother became friends," said Harpen. "He would often ride

the bus to our house after school—we had a big family and he just had
his sister. He was really hyper, today he probably would be put on three
kinds of medicine. But he was very smart, his mind was probably going
90 miles an hour. He was a very sweet kid. He got to be almost like a
brother to me."

Some summers, the Clooney family would spend time with Nick at
work. When George was about eight years old, he spent the summer
hanging about Nick's variety show studio, paying very close attention
to what was going on there. Entertainment was more than just a part of
young Clooney's dad's life; it became part of who he himself was.

"He took more than a 'yeah, this is what my dad does' attitude. He
was interested in the technical part of running a live TV show. I remember coming home and telling my parents, 'That kid really is special, he's
going to be a heartbreaker.' He always had more than a passing interest,
he had a keen eye for what was going on—he was very observant for
a kid. He was involved in the show-biz side, and the technical side as
well," said Mary Ellen Tanner, a singer on the show.[14] She added, "He
was a prankster even then—he was just a funny kid. I remember, I have
this one vision in my mind, he was leaving the studio and I was there,
he smiled that smile and waved at me. I don't know why that stayed
with me all these years."[15]

Another summer, the whole family would awaken at 4:30 A.M. and
drive with Nick to Channel 12, where he hosted his variety show. Nick
would go on to WCKY for his 6–10 A.M. radio show, return to Channel
12 for the variety show, and later host the afternoon movie. George
would play baseball in the halls of Channel 12; then, at night, the
family would drive to Harrison for a play at Beef 'n' Boards, a dinner
theater, where Nina and the children would play in a trailer nearby.[16]

"My father was a workaholic," Clooney said. "Most people I know
are workaholics because when you get the work, you take it. My dad
had five full-time jobs at the same time in 1975. He had a 6 to 10 A.M.
radio show, then a variety show from 11 to 12, then the 3:30 Monday
movie, then he was in a play every night and going away on weekends
and doing this bad game show called *The Money Maze*. He was working nonstop. It almost killed him. It was because the opportunities are
there."[17]

His father's example proved to be a potent one. Many years later and many thousands of miles to the west, Clooney would emulate his father's work schedule as he, too, took up nearly every opportunity presented to him. But years before that drive blossomed, George was a fun-loving kid in small town Ohio with no discernable direction other than the vague assumption that he would be famous.

Mason, Ohio, is a suburb of Cincinnati, about 20 miles from downtown, with approximately 30,000 people. But when the Clooneys moved there, it was a small town of 5,000.

Perry Denehy, who with Pete Harpen and George made a solid trio throughout grade school, remembered that, when the Clooneys moved to Mason in 1969, everyone knew who Nick Clooney was. But, once the students got to know the family, they were considered much like everyone else—albeit with a famous head of household. The Clooneys lived on a farm in Mason, though someone else farmed the property. They lived in a "big old farm house," remembered Denehy, who was in George's fourth-grade class at Western Row. Everyone enjoyed hanging out at the Clooneys' house, spending the day riding bicycles, playing baseball, and exploring the barn.

"We would go to his room and even then there were theatrics—rubber chickens and magic props. George was always animated—he was going to do a skit, going to do a play," said Denehy, who hung out with George until his family moved to Augusta, Kentucky, during eighth grade. "Most of us knew he was destined to follow something in entertainment. Several of us competed to be the class clown, stealing each other's jokes. He thought he was the class clown, but we gave him a run for it!"[18]

By sixth grade, George apparently had won the title of class clown, at least as Barb Wesseler remembers it. Wesseler was George's social studies teacher at St. Susanna Parish School in Mason, where George transferred as soon as there was space. Clooney's class of about 35 students was a good class of kids who spent their free time going on hayrides and having bonfires, said Wesseler, who sometimes went along.

The Clooneys usually sat in the same place at the back of the church, and when friends would walk in, they would pat Nick on the back by way of saying hi, said Wesseler. "They were just normal citizens of Mason—

everyone knew the dad did things with radio and TV, and they performed at Beef 'n' Boards, a dinner theater. People around here would go
see them in the shows and Nina's mother would stay with the kids."[19]

One year, George was in Wesseler's homeroom class. She remembers
him as a fun-loving, well-mannered typical boy—if he could get out of
something, he would.

"He was sort of a Tom Sawyer, getting someone to take his job!"
Wesseler said. "He was not the tall, dark, and handsome kid the girls
swooned over, he was more of their friend—he was the average-size
boy and had reddish-brown hair. In the yearbook, he's wearing it below
his earlobes in a Dutch Boy cut. He claims his first kiss was behind our
church in seventh grade."[20]

At parent-teacher conferences with George's parents, Wesseler would
report that George had satisfactory grades—the school used words such
as "satisfactory" instead of letters in grading—and he progressed from
level to level. If she had anything to tell Nick and Nina Clooney, they
"never disbelieved the teacher"; they'd just write it down.

Megastar George Clooney isn't much different from the boy Wesseler remembered in her classroom.

"You know how he always has the last word in interviews? He did
that. And when he talks, he brushes his thumb against the side of his
face? He used to do that in the sixth grade.

"He always had that little jokey way of answering, too," she continued. "I once saw him on an interview when he was showing people
around his Italian villa. Someone asked the Italian-speaking maids if
he was a nice boss and he said to the maids, 'Say yes, here's another
5,000 lire!' That was typical George from when he was a kid, teasing
people. He always had something cute to say."[21]

Already following in his father's footsteps, Clooney and his friends
Pete and Perry emceed all of the school plays; they also emceed curricu-
lum night, during which every grade performed, for three years straight.
When the parish held a celebration, the trio emceed that, as well.

Wesseler, now media specialist at St. Susanna, has a photo of the
adult Clooney hanging in the media office—one taken while he was
portraying Dr. Doug Ross on ER, wearing scrubs and with a stethoscope
around his neck. It was sold at an auction at the school and is signed by
Clooney, "Thanks for supporting my old school, St. Susanna."[22]

After Wesseler became media specialist, in 1990, she was sorting books in the library, and some of the students found cards with Clooney's name written on them, left over from the day when books were checked out by having a stamped, dated card stuck into a pocket inside the book cover, instead of with a computer.

"He was a reader—we found several of them. We had one framed, and it's hanging here now. George was a library user and was in here a lot," said Wesseler.

But he spent at least as much time playing sports. Clooney was a competitive kid who didn't like to lose. And, though he might have been a reader, no one ever called young George (or older George, for that matter) quiet. Nick Clooney answered this column question about his son as a child: "Was George calm and quiet or loud like me?" asked Sam Williams. Wrote Nick, "He was just like you, Sam."[23]

Did George get along with his sister, Ada, who was almost exactly a year older than he was? "Just like every other brother and sister."[24]

For her part, Ada said, "The kid was the bane of my existence as I was growing up. And so, while I can look at him and say he's quite attractive, I do have some difficulty with my friends saying, 'Oh, he's such a doll!'"[25]

George considered his family life somewhat strict. While he claimed that his father was liberal politically, he noted that his father could be tough on his children. He recalled his mother being a bit more lenient but still demanding. Both of his parents, he remembered, had high expectations for their kids.[26]

When Nick and Nina decided to leave Mason to move to Augusta, Kentucky, their friends were sorry to see the family leave.

"George came up to me and said, 'Why don't you have a going away party for me?'" Denehy said.[27]

He asked his parents' permission, and the party was held in his family's basement, complete with pogo sticks and ping pong. "My mom later felt bad—she said if she would have known he was going to be famous, she would have bought the higher quality hot dogs instead of the cheap generics."

In 1974, with George starting eighth grade and Ada starting high school, it was an opportune time for the Clooneys to move, since they wanted to put down roots after their years of moving around. Nick had been working in Cincinnati, where he was quite well known ("He was Elvis and Johnny Carson," George said),[28] but the couple didn't want to raise their children in a big city. Instead, they looked around several small towns in Kentucky, the state they both came from.

Nina Clooney wrote "It was clear that their work would continue to take them far afield, but they decided to establish a stable home base. After much searching, they chose Augusta, Kentucky, not only for its beauty but also to enable their children to experience the small-town life they had known, Nick in Maysville and Nina in Perryville. The move was everything they hoped. Both children excelled in school and gained confidence in their own abilities in many aspects of real life."[29]

Augusta was a small town of approximately 1,500 people, on the Ohio River. Nick had grown up 16 miles up the river in Maysville, but to move there would have meant even a longer commute for Nick to his job in Cincinnati; as it was, he commuted 45 miles each way to work for many years.

"We drove all around to find a place away from the city," Nick said. "We wanted some sort of a Jeffersonian environment where the children might grow up with a sense of self. It seemed a good idea, and something worked—they're good kids."[30]

In Augusta, the children grew up knowing "poor people, rich people, people in between. A small town like this cuts across every background, every stratification. I don't think you get that in a subdivision."[31]

The Clooneys bought a Victorian home, built in 1898, with a front porch. Over the years, George Clooney has spoken fondly of the town he grew up in. At the time, however, he didn't want to move, and he missed his friends.

George missed St. Susanna so much that he made his way back to Mason for eighth-grade graduation, posing with his old friends in their class picture. "I have no idea how he did that," Nina said. "But there he is in the picture. He's wearing an open-collar shirt and the rest of the boys are in jackets and ties."[32]

Ah, well, he'd grow up to be on several best-dressed lists nonetheless.

Augusta, Kentucky, is a small town where everyone knows everyone. "Augusta says a lot about George's character," said Heather French,

Miss America 2000 and a longtime Clooney family friend. "No wonder when you hear what a great guy he is—he is from Augusta. If you got in trouble there, your parents knew before you got home."[33]

When living in Mason, George had hoped that someday he'd attend Moeller High School and be on the school's state champion football team. But Augusta High School was too small for a football team. He'd joke about it later, saying, "I got traded to Augusta." But the move wasn't easy for him.

It was about then that Clooney developed Bell's palsy, which partially paralyzes the face. For the year he suffered from the condition, Clooney's left eye closed, and he was unable to eat or drink properly. His nickname, he said was Frankenstein. "That was the worst time of my life," he said. "You know how cruel kids can be. I was mocked and taunted, but the experience made me stronger."[34]

Clooney added, "It helped me develop more of a personality. You have to make fun of yourself, or else you're going to have a really rough life."[35] Easy for him to say as an adult, but back then, after losing his old friends and his chance to play football, it was not a fun time. But it might explain his lifelong attachment to another sport.

"He wasn't a happy camper," his mother said. Then he discovered basketball. "He had never played basketball in his life. But he was one of the tallest kids in the class. He's played basketball ever since."[36]

Clooney played baseball and basketball for the Panthers teams. Answering a question in his newspaper column years later, Nick told a child who asked if George still liked to play basketball, "It's the closest thing he has to an obsession, I think. He still plays every day."[37]

When he was in high school, the other sport he enjoyed often was tennis, playing against one of the better tennis players in the area, Ron French. Ron's daughter, Heather, was a little girl in those days and remembers hanging around the tennis court when her dad and George would play.

"George was widely known throughout Augusta as funny and easy to get along with," said Heather. "My parents started a tennis league in the area, and he and George were both very competitive. They were like players who had the same type of competitive spirit and got along well on the tennis court—they were both very into winning. They played together from the time we moved there."[38]

While the parents played mixed doubles at the tennis courts, George would "pal around with the kids," said French. "He is a kid-oriented kind of guy. You can tell that when he's with his niece and nephew, Allison and Nicky. He would pal around with us and tease us—I had long hair and pigtails and he'd call me 'Peggy Sue' or 'Piggy Sue' and pull my pigtails. Then I'd kick him."

Years later, when George was living in Hollywood but still able to come back to Augusta often, French remembers seeing him at festivals and playing basketball in the park. Then she saw him after she was crowned Miss Kentucky.

"I attended a dinner in Lexington where the Clooney family was getting an award and my brother said, 'George wants to see you.' The first thing he says is, 'I still have bruises on my shin!' The thing you really want George Clooney to remember about you is that you used to kick him! I was working on my master's and I was Miss Kentucky, but, oh, great! He was always the big brother."[39]

Nick Clooney wrote about that same conversation in one of his columns, after noting that Heather French brought her Miss Kentucky title back to Augusta and Maysville after her win: "She was gracious and had an attractive self-deprecation about all of the fuss."[40] Must be a local trait.

George went to his high school Prom with Laura Laycock, now Laura Bach. Even then, George was the perpetual cut-up, she says. "George teased people and did imitations of friends," she adds. "It was just part of George goofing around. George was a typical teenager. We decided to go together just to have fun. I was kind of like a tomboy. We palled around."[41]

Finally—one meaningful difference between Clooney the kid and Clooney the adult: his one-time lack of pull on women. Just one change, but it was a big one.

NOTES

1. Staff and wire reports, "Rosie Talks about 54 Years of Show Business," *Cincinnati Post*, September 23, 1999, Perspective Extra 18.

2. Joel Stein, "Guess Who Came to Dinner?" *Time*, March 3, 2008, p. 46.

3. Clarissa Cruz, "By George He's Got It—The Ocean's Eleven Star Proves He's Head of the Hollywood Class," *Entertainment Weekly*, December 14, 2001, p. 10.

4. *Larry King Live*, CNN, February 17, 2006.

5. Jeryl Brunner, "What's Your Treasure? One Kid's Junk Is Another One's Gem. Stars Reveal the Personal Possessions They Cherished as Kids," *In Style*, May 1, 2003, p. 307.

6. Anne-Marie O'Neill, "Boy George—At 40, George Clooney Seems as Committed as Ever to His Buddies, Basketball, a Certain Potbellied Pig—And Bachelorhood," *People*, May 7, 2001, p. 96.

7. Cynthia Sanz, "Sexiest Man Alive 1997/George Clooney," *People*, November 17, 1997, p. 77.

8. Dotson Rader, "It's Finally about Friendship and Loyalty," *Parade*, June 7, 1998, p. 4.

9. Debra Ann Vance, "They Can Prove They Know George," *Cincinnati Post*, September 19, 1997, p. 14A.

10. Author's phone interview with Carol Rauch, October 16, 2008.

11. Ibid.

12. Margaret A. McGurk and John Kiesewetter, "Curious, Funny, Ambitious George," *Cincinnati Enquirer*, March 5, 2006, p. 1I.

13. Anne Harpen, phone interview with author, October 30, 2008.

14. Mary Elley Tanner, phone interview with author, October 23, 2008.

15. Ibid.

16. John Kiesewetter, *Cincinnati Enquirer*, November 13, 1985, p. D1.

17. Craig Kopp, *Cincinnati Post*, June 25, 1998, Perspective 16.

18. Perry Denehy, phone interview with author, February 27, 2008.

19. Barb Wesseler, phone interview with author, March 14, 2008.

20. Ibid.

21. Ibid.

22. Ibid.

23. Nick Clooney, "A Few Answers for Curious Kids," *Cincinnati Post*, May 5, 1999, p. 1C.

24. Ibid.

25. McGurk and Kiesewetter, "Curious, Funny, Ambitious George."

26. Rader, "It's Finally about Friendship and Loyalty."

27. Perry Denehy, phone interview with author, February 27, 2008.

28. Ian Parker, "Somebody Has to Be in Control," *New Yorker*, April 14, 2008, p. 40.

29. Nina Clooney, "George Clooney," in *Encyclopedia of Northern Kentucky* (Lexington: The University Press of Kentucky, 2009).

30. Bettye Lee Mastin, "Kentucky Ties Bring Clooneys Back Home," *Lexington Herald-Leader*, April 19, 1987, p. E1.

31. Ibid.

32. Ibid.

33. Heather French, phone interview with author, September 3, 2008.

34. *The Mirror,* 2003, http://www.people.com/people/george_clooney; the biography is at bottom of the page.

35. *W.,* December 2007.

36. *The Mirror,* 2003, http://www.people.com/people/george_clooney.

37. Nick Clooney, "Students Keep Letters Coming," *Cincinnati Post,* May 20, 1998, p. 1C.

38. Heather French, phone interview with author, September 3, 2008.

39. Ibid.

40. Nick Clooney, "Old Friendships Bring Satisfaction," *Cincinnati Post,* September 22, 1999, p. 1C.

41. *People,* May 27, 1996, p. 42.

Chapter 2

EVERYONE'S FAMOUS

While most people are somewhat influenced by their family, George Clooney seems to have been affected by his more than most. He grew up in a home where famous people were just regular people, where entertaining was part of the family culture, where conversation typically included discussion of what was going on in the world.

Watching Aunt Rosemary's fame peak and ebb when he was a boy, George learned lessons few future celebrities know ahead of time: that while his aunt's voice had not faltered, the world of music had changed, that fame was fleeting and not something to be counted on or taken too seriously. It was clearly a Clooney tradition to stick close to your roots, to stay connected to the people who raised you and grew up with you, and to help improve the world around you.

To understand George Clooney, one needs to understand the five people closest to him, particularly the two men in his life: his father, Nick, and his great-uncle and godfather, his father's uncle, for whom he was named—George Guilfoyle.

NICK CLOONEY

Someone who writes a newspaper column for 15 years can't help but divulge a lot about himself. Nick Clooney is no exception. The pasta and jazz fan has said that his favorite writer was Mark Twain and that listening to Edward R. Murrow and Peter Grant on the radio as a little boy inspired him to be a broadcaster.[1]

He has been a writer as long as he can remember—at the age of five, he wrote lyrics to a song his sister, Rosemary, used to sing to family.[2] Fame has been part of Nick's life for all but the first few years, considering that he was 10 when his two sisters, Betty and Rosemary, became well-known singers on local radio station WLW and 15 when Rosemary's breakout hit, *Come on-a My House* hit the top of the record charts. A child once wrote to Nick and asked if, as a child, he thought he'd be famous. Surprisingly, his answer was yes.[3] Coincidentally, or not, George Clooney also has often said he somehow knew he'd be famous some day.

"I got used to being Rosemary Clooney's brother," Nick wrote. "I had plenty of time to get used to that because it lasted until I was middle-aged. Then, when 'ER' struck TV gold, I got used to being George Clooney's father."[4]

Nicholas Joseph Clooney was born January 13, 1934, in Maysville, Kentucky. His parents divorced when Nick was four, and his father wasn't around much after that. He grew up in a family of people who worked at regular jobs, from entrepreneur to farmers.[5] Nick's mother, Frances Guilfoyle Clooney, found work in Cincinnati after the divorce, while he and his sisters stayed in Maysville with their grandmother, where they enjoyed spending time listening to the radio. Nick and his sisters grew up entertaining. He remembers talking into a tin can, emulating news announcers, while Rosemary and Betty sang.[6]

"We'd come out of the Russell Theater on Saturday after the double feature, we would be whoever was on the screen. Then Sunday we would put on a show," said Nick.[7]

Performing was ingrained in the Clooney clan. Nick's Aunt Annabelle Guilfoyle sang at the Club Casano in Cincinnati, and his father, Andy Clooney, played the mandolin for friends. His aunt Olivette Clooney played piano on the radio, and his grandmother and uncles sang hymns for the family. When the group gathered, a variety show broke out.[8]

When his sisters were 16 and 13, their hobby became a job. When Rosemary's career took off and she became a singing sensation, his family was affected in ways none of them could have imagined.[9]

"The cover of every magazine required a story, the story required a quote, a quote required us. We learned fast. Subtly, but irrevocably, our lives changed. The stakes were raised. So were expectations. Though most of us would deny it publicly, we required more of ourselves. Nick wrote."[10]

When Nick was 16, in August 1951, he got a job at Maysville radio station WFTM.[11] He introduced and announced concerts for his older sisters, as well. It was a perfect fit—the girls loved music and songs, while Nick's lifelong passion had been imitating radio announcers like Elmer Davis and Ed Murrow.[12] Though being Rosemary's brother certainly could have been something impressive to mention to prospective employers, Nick not only hesitated to mention his sister but tried to distance his career from hers—much in the way his son would later choose to distance his career aspirations from his famous father's.

"It was a problem in my mind, when I was a teenager, to the point where I wouldn't play any of Rosemary's records. She was so ticked at me that wherever I was, I wasn't playing her. That, of course, was stupid, but it seemed important at the time."[13]

Nick graduated from St. Patrick High School in Maysville in 1952. He took a job at a Delaware station two years later anchoring the news; the 18-year-old was told, "The news starts at 11 and ends when you've told people what they need to know."[14]

During a visit to his sister at Paramount Studios, he was asked to do a screen test for Cecil B. DeMille. Though he was a handsome young man—not unlike his actor son—his voice didn't match his youth. "You look like you're 19 and you sound like you're 35," DeMille told him. "My guess is you'll have great difficulty if you want to become an actor until you look like you sound."[15]

When Nick was drafted, he worked as a reporter for Armed Forces Radio in Germany. Two years later, Nick returned to the United States and to Hollywood, where, in 1957, he spent about a year doing bit movie parts. He auditioned for the lead in *I Was a Teenage Werewolf* but lost out to Michael Landon. He did appear in a movie with Dean Jones, *Handle with Care*, and a dog food commercial, but he soon returned to Kentucky to work for WLAP radio in Lexington.

"I never thought of myself as an actor," Nick Clooney said. "It is very difficult. You have to be someone else. I don't know how to do that."[16]

He stayed in Lexington for eight years, and the experience literally changed his life. He met Nina Warren at the Miss Lexington contest, which she won. Nick, at the contest because of his duties at the station, has said he was immediately "smitten"; they married in 1959 and had two children there. The couple moved back to Ohio in 1966, and Nick worked at WLW-AM and WSAI-AM. He hosted his own variety show into the 1970s at WLCW in Columbus, then had shows at WCPO-TV and WKRC-TV in Cincinnati.

After several moves in Ohio, Nick and Nina decided to establish a permanent home in Augusta, Kentucky. Nick was hosting both a daily TV talk/variety show and a daily morning radio show in Cincinnati, while on weekends he flew to New York City to tape *The Money Maze*, a daily network game show on ABC-TV.

In 1976, Nick became an anchor and managing editor for WKRC-TV news in Cincinnati. As the news anchor for Channel 12, Nick engineered a locally legendary rise for the program from last place to first in the space of a few years, utilizing two basic ingredients: fairness and accuracy. His popularity as a news anchor was not immediate.

"[Viewers] had every right to say, 'You've been throwing pies at Carol Channing. You are going to tell me what happened in Over-the-Rhine?'" Clooney said. "And they were right. I had to earn that. It was not easy. It was a very tough two years when we were beaten like a drum."[17]

Nick's news background and his insistence on hiring reporters and upgrading equipment helped turn things around. He also benefited from personal characteristics that would often also be attributed to his son in future years—basic decency and civility. Nick's way was to present subjects of the newscast as human beings deserving of the same respect as anyone else, without judging what they had done.

"I can't tell you how many times Nick walked out because something wasn't right, just right. They'd ask him to come back and he'd say, 'I'll do it, if this changes.' Things like inaccurate promos and other things. He was all about ethics," Channel 12 staffer Deborah Dixon said.[18]

Nick went on to anchor newscasts in Los Angeles, Salt Lake City, and Buffalo before returning to Cincinnati radio. In 1989, Nick began writing newspaper columns, which appeared in the *Cincinnati Post* and the *Kentucky Post*, as well as, for a time, the *Maysville* (KY) *Ledger-Independent*. Nick quit as a columnist for the *Ledger-Independent* in 1997 after a writer for that paper, Clinton Burton, wrote a column criticizing George Clooney for "forgetting his roots and rarely returning home— particularly during last March's Ohio River flood." The column elicited letters to the editor in defense of George.[19]

In the late 1980s, Nick hosted a syndicated weekday court show, *On Trial*, and in 1994 he began hosting and writing for American Movie Classics, developing a special interest in film preservation. He also wrote two books in those years: *Cincinnati: A Love Story*, which appeared in 1991, and *Nick*, a collection of columns, published in 1995.

Nick's columns in the *Post* usually dealt with such topics as local politics, history, and his family. As George's career took off, Nick's columns provided a front-row seat to George's star-studded life.

A letter from *Post* reader Stanley Fogle in 1997 suggested as much: "It is rare that the [general public] gets an opportunity to track such meteoric careers from such a connected source. [My family] hopes you will find more frequent opportunities to write about your interesting family, even the members who are not famous."[20]

More than a year later, Nick wrote about his unusual circumstance of having two incredibly famous people in his immediate family over the course of two generations., He wrote about the flip side of fame, at least as he had experienced it by watching two of the people closest to him and how it impacted their lives. Though the common perception was that people who became famous changed the way they acted toward others, Clooney observed a somewhat different effect in a portion of the public—that the way people treated his relatives changed, and quite often not for the better.[21]

In 2002, Nick published *Movies That Changed Us* and began hosting "Moments That Changed Us" on the network American Life TV. Over the years, Nick won many career awards, including "Best in Business of Television News," awarded by the *Washington Journalism Review*; a regional Emmy for commentary; and an honorary doctorate of fine arts from Northern Kentucky University. He was inducted into the Cincinnati Journalism Hall of Fame by the Society of Professional Journalists and received the Distinguished Kentuckian Award from the Kentucky Broadcasters Association.[22]

In June 2002, Nick Clooney was honored for his 50 years in broadcasting at a charity event to benefit the Kidney Foundation of Greater Cincinnati. At "A Night for Nick," four words were used most often to describe the guest of honor: kind, humane, compassionate, and talented. It was a night for everyone to switch roles for a little while. As George Clooney noted, "It is great to come here and just be Nick's kid. Pop has sort of been Rosemary's brother forever, so this is fun for him."[23]

Daughter Ada brought a message from Nick's sister Rosemary, at home recovering from surgery in California. "Congratulations to my little Nicky," Ada read; then she added, "She can get away with saying things like that."[24] Tributes also came in from journalists such as former CNN anchor Bernie Shaw: "You are the broadcaster Edward R. Murrow envisioned—a perennial exception to all else, packaged in walking grace and civility."

From *Dateline NBC* reporter and former Channel 12 reporter Edie Magnus: "He is a man who actually stood for something. It was pure passion when he came to work at Channel 12."

From Walter Cronkite: "He is my kind of guy with a devotion to reporting, writing and broadcasting that far exceeds the norm with humor and the right touch of cynicism."

From Mike Reid, a former Cincinnati Bengal who became a country singer and songwriter and a composer of operas whom Nick had encouraged on his variety show: "Nick, you've always said, 'In order to achieve anything, one must overcome common sense.'"[25]

George's tribute to his father included this: "You have the two most important things you could ever want—the love and admiration of all of your friends, and you have your hair."

George also spoke about his father, using words that have often been used by others to describe George himself: "There's a humanity to him. Everybody has a family and a life and he treats them all that way. He teaches you can still get away with that."[26]

As if to illustrate that point, the entire Clooney family stayed at the Music Hall late into the night to shake hands, sign autographs, and pose for pictures with the catering staff.

At that time, Nick was still hosting a weekday radio show, writing columns for the *Post*, and starting to host on a nostalgia cable network, Goodlife. He also was working to syndicate weekly editions of two radio shows he produced, *Movie Music* and *In the Company of Heroes*, which featured conversations with war veterans.

"People in my business don't retire," Nick said. "They get retired. As long as people keep calling and say will you show up here and do this. That is what I've been doing since I was 16."[27]

A year and a half later, someone asked him to show up and do something entirely different—run for Congress, for the seat left open by the retirement of three-term Democratic Kentucky congressman Ken Lucas. Clooney told reporters he began discussing the possibility with Lucas in August 2003 after Lucas told him he would honor his term-limit pledge if he felt there was another Democrat who would run for the seat and had a shot at winning. He believed Clooney, 69, was that person.

In a statement, Lucas said Clooney was "a fresh face on the political scene who is intelligent, articulate, highly respected and, above all, passionate about standing up for his beliefs and the people of his district." Though Clooney had turned down offers to run for Congress and the governor's office in the past, he said the timing was right: "My family and I determined that it would be a proper next step for us to enter the arena of politics on which we had commented for so many years."[28]

The race was not to be an easy one. Lucas, who had held his seat for three terms, was the only Democrat in Kentucky's eight-member congressional delegation. Three Republicans entered the primary to reclaim the seat that had been the party's for 30 years before Lucas won it in 1998. It was also to be an expensive race. When asked if George would help with fundraising, Nick replied, "I certainly hope my son will contribute the $2,000 allowed."[29] George did help with fundraising, including appearing at a $1,000-a-person get-together at a private home and a $250-a-person reception at a restaurant.

Nick's opponent in the general election was business consultant Geoff Davis, who had narrowly lost to Lucas two years before. A year after Nick announced his candidacy, he lost the race for the Fourth District's seat in the U.S. House of Representatives to Davis on November 3, 2004. Davis received approximately 55 percent of the vote.

Pundits suggested that Clooney's liberal politics, as evidenced in his many newspaper columns over the years, didn't fly with the majority of the voters in the district.

After the election, Nick returned to the *Post* to continue writing columns until the paper closed on December 31, 2007. He also traveled to Darfur with George to make a documentary, *A Journey to Darfur*, about the genocide in the wartorn region of Sudan. In 2008, Nick—who had had no formal education since graduating from high school in 1952—accepted a two-day-a-week position as a "distinguished journalist in residence" at Washington, D.C.'s American University. The appointment was part of a partnership between American University's (AU) School of Communication and the Newseum, an interactive museum of news where Nick worked one day a week and above which he and his wife kept an apartment while Nick worked at AU. He taught opinion writing in the fall and in the spring taught a course titled "Films That Changed Us," which he based on his book *Movies That Changed Us: Reflections on the Screen*. His book analyzed the significance of classics such as *The Birth of a Nation*, *The Jazz Singer*, *Dr. Strangelove*, *Stagecoach*, *The Graduate*, *Star Wars*, and *Saving Private Ryan*.

"Nick Clooney is a natural fit for AU's School of Communication," said the school's dean, Larry Kirkman, in a press release about the appointment. "His professional experiences bridge all three of our academic divisions: journalism, public communication and film and media arts."

The biggest change for Nick with his newest job wasn't as much the teaching as it was the requirement that he establish an e-mail address.[30] "In a high-def world, I am an analog guy," Clooney said. "All the years I wrote for the *Post*, I wrote the first draft in longhand, typed the second and faxed it in."[31]

But after he accepted the job at AU, officials asked for his e-mail address. When he said he didn't have one, they said he'd have to get one to communicate with his students. So, he bought a laptop and took computer lessons from a neighbor.[32]

When Clooney began teaching his course, he went through the syllabus with his class, including the list of guest lecturers—which did not include his famous son. "He's too expensive for me," Clooney joked. "He has to keep working, because he's my retirement plan."[33]

As it turned out, son George did appear at the School of Communication in January 2009 as part of Clooney's "Reel Journalism" film series at the Newseum. The series presents movies that depict journalists and journalism, providing a forum for discussing the role of media in a democratic society. The series was planned to continue through at least the fall of 2009.

Retirement did not seem to be in Nick's vocabulary, actually. In addition to his work as a professor, he continued to write, produce, and host the American Life TV Network series *Moments That Changed Us*, for which he interviewed such newsmakers as John Glenn, Walter Cronkite, and Diahann Carroll.

Cincinnati sports anchor Denny Janson, who worked with Clooney for years, wasn't surprised at Nick's busy schedule into his mid-70s. "Work is Nick's passion," Janson said. "He doesn't play golf. He doesn't sculpt. He works. He is one of the more purposeful people I've ever met."[34]

Friends and colleagues of Nick's son have often made similar observations about George. So much of who George Clooney is can be easily traced back to the father whose ideas about politics and news seeped in to the very being of his son—the son who eventually would bring to the silver screen the story of his father's hero, Edward R. Murrow, and do it so well.

"As proud of my father was of Murrow, that's how proud I am of my dad," George said.[35]

GEORGE WESLEY GUILFOYLE

Nick Clooney once wrote, "Some individuals are marked from birth to be unique. To be the one others copy, admire, talk about. These are the people who are welcomed when they arrive and missed when they leave. George has always been one of these."[36]

He was writing not about his son George but about his Uncle George, the man whose name he gave to his only son, His beloved Uncle George stood in for the father who was rarely in Nick's life, teaching Nick the sorts of lessons a father usually teaches his son.

George Wesley Guilfoyle was Nick's mother's younger brother, a teenager when Nick was born. George's older brothers got jobs and got married, and Nick became George's de facto little brother. When Guilfoyle graduated from high school, rather than take a scholarship to Xavier University, he went to work to support his sister's family. He got a job at Baldwin Piano, and the family moved from Maysville to Cincinnati.

When World War II broke out, George took the test for aviation cadets, passed it, and became a B-17 pilot after a friend told him he'd never pass the test. He flew a couple of dozen missions over Europe. When the war was over, Nick, though just a kid, could tell that his uncle George wasn't the same; George and his best friend, Phil, both not quite 24, "would never laugh in quite the same way again," Nick wrote.[37]

Guilfoyle returned home to find that Nick's sisters, Rosemary and Betty, who were singing on the radio, had been offered jobs as singers with Tony Pastor's band. But, if they were to travel around the country and have a chance to become stars, they'd need a relative to become their legal guardian and manager and travel with them. So George became their manager, watching over the siblings (and teaching all three, including Nick, how to drive) until Rosemary's success and both girls' marriages.[38]

In later years, George found his own passion—horses. He taught himself to train horses and spent years doing just that. Though he had dated many women, he never found the right time to marry. He died in July 1990, and all of his nieces and nephews remember him with overwhelming affection.[39] This includes George Clooney, who didn't know George Guilfoyle until he trained horses, became a drunk, and slept in a barn.[40] George was sorry he'd missed the years of Guilfoyle's youth, when he was a fun-loving all-star basketball player who dated Miss America.[41] He fondly remembers Guilfoyle as someone who could tell captivating stories and was great with kids, though he wasn't conventionally successful.[42]

Guilfoyle's influence on his nephew is undeniable. Besides the fact that stories about Uncle George in the 1950s sound somewhat like stories told about George Clooney today (the bachelor with a great sense of humor who loved children and was an exceptional uncle), there is a sense that, at a couple of points in his life, the younger George might not have lived up to his potential but for the cautionary tale of his uncle's unfulfilled promise.

When Guilfoyle died, of cancer, in 1990, the not-yet-successful George Clooney was holding his hand.[43]

ROSEMARY CLOONEY

Great-uncle George provided just one of George Clooney's lessons on success. The opposite experiences of his Aunt Rosemary provided the other.

Rosemary Clooney, daughter of Andrew and Frances Guilfoyle Clooney, was raised in her grandmother's house with her siblings, Nick and Betty, in Maysville, Kentucky. Her mother was a seamstress in retail shops; her father was a house painter. They divorced when Rosemary was a teenager.

When Rosemary was 16 and her sister was not quite 14, they won a singing contest to appear on Cincinnati's far-reaching WLW radio. Within a year, they were touring with the Tony Pastor band, with their Uncle George Guilfoyle chaperoning them.

Betty resigned after a few years, and Rosemary went on to a solo career in 1949 and a recording contract with Columbia Records in New York City. Her records were enormously successful, selling millions, and she appeared in nightclubs and on TV shows. On one of the shows, she met her future husband, actor-producer-director Jose Ferrer.

In 1951, she recorded one of her biggest hits, *Come on-a My House*. Two years later, her first motion picture, *The Stars Are Singing*, premiered at the Russell Theater in Maysville and she married Ferrer (eventually the couple had five children). In 1954, she was cast in the now classic *White Christmas*, with Bing Crosby and Danny Kaye. *The Rosemary Clooney Show*, a half-hour syndicated show, debuted on TV in 1956.

In 1968, Rosemary suffered a nervous breakdown. It was widely attributed to "family challenges and to witnessing the assassination of her close friend Robert F. Kennedy,"[44] but Clooney was known to suffer from depression and drug addiction as well. In later years, Rosemary sang occasionally at small supper clubs, recorded two dozen albums of mainly American standards, and, in 1997, married her longtime companion, Dante DiPaolo. The wedding was at St. Patrick Catholic Church in Maysville, where Rosemary had been baptized as a baby.

The big event was the highlight of the year in Maysville, and Rose-mary—no matter how big a star she was—wanted no traces of Holly-wood there. Her photographer was the son of an old school friend. The cake was baked by Magee's, which had baked birthday cakes for the Clooney family since Nick, Rosemary, and Betty were children; they'd created the cake for the wedding of Nick's daughter, Ada.

Cake decorator Judy Dickson told the *Cincinnati Post* days before Rosemary's wedding that her cake was "A traditional stacked cake, but it wouldn't be right to tell everybody what it's like before she sees it." So, true to the Maysville spirit of loyalty, she didn't.[45]

Mary Ellen Tanner, a Cincinnati singer who met Rosemary after per-forming on Nick's variety show, attended the wedding and noted that Cincinnati food was featured at the reception—Graeter's ice cream, White Castle hamburgers (Mary Ellen heard fashion designer Bob Mackey ask, "What are *those?*") and, of course, Magee's cakes.

The highlight of the day, Tanner remembered, was watching Bob and Dolores Hope arrive a little late.

"They went through hell and high water to get there—you don't just get a jet to Maysville. We all cried—it was such history there, that old couple. He really enjoyed the Montgomery Inn ribs!"[46]

Sadly, it wouldn't be too many years before the next time Maysville honored Rosemary at the same church—at her funeral in 2002. Ten pallbearers—sons, grandsons, and nephew George Clooney—would carry the coffin afterward. The 74-year-old died after six-month battle with lung cancer. One of Rosemary's doctors from the Mayo Clinic in Rochester, Minnesota, attended the funeral, saying she had been im-pressed with the singer's spirit. Rosemary always thought about those around her, no matter how sick she was.[47]

Tanner was asked to sing at a gathering after Rosemary's funeral. She remembers the hot day well.

"It was 100 degrees in the shade and Nick was sitting not more than 20 feet from me, holding his dog. He looked so hurt, he loved his sisters so much. Then George came up and put his arms around his dad. I could hardly sing, it was a very emotional day."[48]

It was emotional for many people. Maysville residents and those from surrounding communities lined the streets to watch the procession to the cemetery, people stopping whatever they were doing to pay tribute to their hometown idol, Rosemary Clooney. Children held flowers, and police officers stood at attention.[49]

"She never really lost her Maysville roots," Dick Murgatroyd, a former WLWT-TV producer, said. "She had a small-town feeling. She treated everyone that way, wherever she was."[50]

Nephew George Clooney stayed out of sight most of the day, declining interviews. His only public comment about the aunt who allowed him to move into her home when he first arrived in Hollywood was, "She was a great lady."

Rosemary and her nephew, George, were very close, said Heather French, a family friend who adored Rosemary. "I took a lot of inspiration from their family. Augusta had never had a Miss America, and Rosemary taught me never to forget where I came from," said Miss America 2000 who, with her husband, former Kentucky Lieutenant Governor Steve Henry, maintains the Rosemary Clooney house and museum in Augusta. "She was so concerned about me being a small town girl making it big. She told me, 'I know what it's like.' She was so real and had such a sense of humor—she was a great friend."[51]

NINA WARREN CLOONEY

Nina Warren, born on August 24, 1939, was eight years old before her family had electricity at her home, and she had no indoor plumbing until after she married and moved out. She rarely saw movies as a child, but, during some summers, a man would come to Perryville, Kentucky, where she lived, and show movies outside, using the wall of a warehouse as a screen. Nina thought about those days in amazement at how far the world had come right after she and her husband watched on TV as their son won an Academy Award.[52]

Her family wasn't quite like Nick's; her family members were mostly farmers. When Nina was a teenager, she won several beauty pageants, which she entered to earn money for college tuition. She began with county fairs and eventually was crowned Miss Lexington and then first runner-up to Miss Kentucky. Nick often wrote, "She is just slightly prettier now than she was then."[53]

During the Miss Lexington pageant, Nina, a student at the University of Kentucky, met local broadcaster Nick Clooney. Nina won the contest, sponsored partly by his station, and it was Nick's job as the station's representative to escort the new Miss Lexington to various functions.

Nick popped the question before the two knew each other well at all, according to a writer who owned the home they rented in Mason. "At a civic dinner, still before they had actually gone out together, Nick said to her, 'Would you pass the butter, please, and would you marry me?' Nina, with the aplomb that carries her through both public and private life, replied without missing a beat, 'Here's the butter, and yes.'"[54] They married and had both of their children before leaving Lexington in 1966.[55]

Nina has described herself as "a writer, inventor and television host."[56] She has owned an antique store in Augusta, served on the city council there, handled Nick's bookings, received a design patent for a new type of bag for carry-out food, designed a park in Augusta, and worked in television. She is on the board of directors of the Maysville Community College and of a proposed outdoor drama center near Augusta. She used to pinch-hit for Nick when he was unable to write his newspaper column and has recently written a not-yet-released book, *And His Lovely Wife, Nina.*

"Nina Clooney is probably one of the most lovely women I've ever met in my life," says Miss America 2000 and family friend Heather French.[57]

ADA CLOONEY ZEIDLER

Born almost exactly a year before her famous brother, in May 1960, Ada Clooney Zeidler prefers not to use her real name, Adelia. She was named after Nick Clooney's grandmother Adelia Guilfoyle. Ada was class president at Augusta High School, the co-lead in the senior play, and the only Merit Scholar from the school in 1978. Ada's husband, Norman, a Gulf War veteran, died in 2004 at the age of 47. She is an accountant—she chose accounting as a anti-Clooney profession, joking, "You're all crazy—somebody has to do something practical"— and the mother of two children, Allison and Nickie.[58]

"She was never bitten by the bug to perform or be a broadcaster or journalist. Still, I think she one day will write the family story. She's the smartest of us," her father wrote.[59]

"She's very proud of George," says French. "She's always there at any event, and she also campaigned for her dad. I don't ever get the feeling she wanted to go down the road George is going down. But whenever I hear about George not having children—he goes all out for Allison and Nickie, he thinks the world of them and they think the world of him."[60]

NOTES

1. Nick Clooney, "A Few Answers for Curious Kids," *Cincinnati Post*, May 5, 1999, p. 1C.

2. Ibid.

3. Ibid.

4. Nick Clooney, "Now I'm Sleeping with the Politician," *Cincinnati Post*, November 8, 1996, p. 1C.

5. Nick Clooney, "Fame Creates New Tensions," *Cincinnati Post*, May 8, 1998, p. 1C.

6. Rick Bird, "A Tribute to Nick Clooney: 50 Years in Broadcasting," *Cincinnati Post*, June 6, 2002, p.1B.

7. Ibid.

8. Nick Clooney, "Hollywood Fetes Clooneys," *Cincinnati Post*, October 4, 1996, p. 1B.

9. Clooney, "Fame Creates New Tensions."

10. Ibid.

11. Nina Clooney, "Nick Clooney," in *Encyclopedia of Northern Kentucky* (Lexington: The University Press of Kentucky, 2009).

12. John Kiesewetter, "Just Call Him 'Professor Clooney,'" *Cincinnati Enquirer*, August 23, 2008, p. A1.

13. Bird, "A Tribute to Nick Clooney."

14. Ibid.

15. John Kiesewetter, "A Closer Look at Nick Clooney," *Cincinnati Enquirer*, June 20, 2002, p. E1.

16. Ibid.

17. Ibid.

18. Ibid.

19. Jerry Brewer, "Maysville Residents Angry over Article Criticizing Clooney," *Lexington Herald-Leader*, June 4, 1997, p. A1.

20. Nick Clooney "Catching up on Holiday Mail," *Cincinnati Post*, January 20, 1997, p.1B.

21. Clooney, "Fame Creates New Tensions."

22. Clooney, "Nick Clooney."

23. Ibid.

24. Rick Bird, "World's Greatest Honor Clooney," *Cincinnati Post*, June 24, 2002, p. X1B.

25. Ibid.

26. Ibid.

27. Ibid.

28. Michael Collins, "It's Clooney for Congress: Yep, Nick Is Taking a Shot," *Cincinnati Post*, November 24, 2003, p. A1.

29. Ibid.

30. Kiesewetter, "Just Call Him 'Professor Clooney.'"

31. Ibid.

32. Ibid.

33. Ibid.

34. Ibid.

35. Margaret A. McGurk and John Kiesewetter, "Curious, Funny, Ambitious George," *Cincinnati Enquirer*, March 5, 2006, p. 1I.

36. Nick Clooney, *Cincinnati Post*, July 23, 1990, p. B1.

37. Nick Clooney, "Uncle George: A Family Man in Every Sense," *Cincinnati Post*, July 23, 1990, p. B1.

38. Ibid.

39. Nick Clooney, "Remembering Two Soldiers and Pals," *Cincinnati Post*, May 31, 1999, p. 1C.

40. Nick Clooney, "Rosie's First Car Was a De Soto," *Cincinnati Post*, July 31, 2002, p. 1B.

41. Clooney, "Uncle George."

42. Ibid.

43. Dotson Rader, "It's Finally about Friendship and Loyalty," *Parade*, June 7, 1998, p. 4.

44. John C. Schlipp, "Fame Came Fast for Clooney Sisters of Maysville," *Cincinnati Post*, January 23, 2006, p. B2.

45. Peggy Kreimer, "A Nice Little Wedding for Maysville's Big Star," *Cincinnati Post*, November 7, 1997, p. 1A.

46. Mary Ellen Tanner, phone interview with author, October 23, 2008.

47. Janelle Gelfand and John Kiesewetter, "Fans, Family Pay Tribute to Rosemary Clooney," *Cincinnati Enquirer*, July 6, 2002, p. 1A.

48. Mary Ellen Tanner, phone interview with author, October 23, 2008.

49. Gelfand and Kiesewetter, "Fans, Family Pay Tribute to Rosemary Clooney."

50. Ibid.

51. Heather French, phone interview with author, September 3, 2008.

52. Nick Clooney, "Reflecting on Oscar, Hard Times," *Cincinnati Post*, February 1, 2006, p. C1.

53. Clooney, "A Few Answers for Curious Kids."

54. Jane Durrell, "At Home with the Clooneys," *Fiftyplus*, May 2002, http://cache.zoominfo.com/CachedPage/?archive_id=0&page_id=306151753&page_url=%2f%2fwww.fifty-plus.com%2farticles%2far0205a.html&page_last_updated=2%2f10%2f2003+10%3a24%3a57+AM&firstName=Nina&lastName=Clooney.

55. Bettye Lee Mastin, "Kentucky Ties Bring Clooneys Back Home," *Lexington Herald-Leader*, April 19, 1987, p. E1.

56 Clooney, "George Clooney."

57. Heather French, phone interview with author, September 3, 2008.

58. Durrell, "At Home with the Clooneys."

59. Nick Clooney, "Students Keep Letters Coming," *Cincinnati Post*, May 20, 1998, p. 1C.

60. Heather French, phone interview with author, September 3, 2008.

Chapter 3

THE ACTING BUG

After graduation, in 1979, from Augusta High School—where George had considered himself a so-so student but a pretty good athlete—he thought he could play baseball for the Cincinnati Reds. He found out he was only lacking one thing: skill.[1] He attended an open tryout and realized what many kids who grow up as a big fish in a small pond realize—he wasn't as good as he thought he was. After accepting his limitations, he felt comfortable walking away from a baseball career, knowing that he had tried.[2]

The 80-mph fastballs weren't too bad, Clooney said, but the 85-mph curveball floored him.

"It was such a clear moment in my mind where I thought, that's a game I don't even understand. And that kid doesn't even pitch in the pros—he pitches in the semi-pros."[3]

With his career in baseball over before it began, Clooney had no plan for his future. He enrolled in college and tried several part-time jobs.[4] His parents lamented his lack of direction, perhaps comparing him to his academically oriented sister. "Actually, I always thought he was going to be in some kind of show business, because of his personality," his mother, Nina, said. "We thought he would be a stand-up comedian."[5]

Whether stand-up comedy wasn't on George's agenda or whether he couldn't make money at it is unknown. Instead, he did what many college students do to make some extra cash—he headed to the local malls. He sold menswear at Nadler's in Kenwood, Ohio, and shoes at McAlpin's in Crestview Hills, Kentucky, where he was very popular with both his coworkers and his customers. He used to draw smiley faces on the soles of shoes he sold and papered the backroom wall with funny sketches of his coworkers.

Virginia Schwartz worked with George in the shoe department at McAlpin's department store. About 30 years older than George, she was "more like a mother" to him than a friend.

"He was in college. He was so nice to work with, he was a lot of fun. He'd draw caricatures of people—he was so good at drawing those. He once drew one on the bottom of a shoe and the girl bought the shoes just because she liked the drawing. He put one on my locker one Halloween," said Schwartz. "He was also really nice to the older people, they all liked him."[6]

Clooney once told Schwartz a story about how he'd been out at his favorite bar, The Conservatory, the night before and seen a truck loaded with watermelons. He took one and put it in his car, and, on the way home, when he hit a bump, the watermelon exploded all over the car.

"I told him that's what you get for stealing a watermelon!"

George used to complain to Schwartz about his father being "on his back."

"I said someday he'll be glad his dad was always on his back," said Schwartz, who still keeps in touch with Clooney when he comes home for a visit.

George attended Northern Kentucky University, just southeast of Cincinnati in Highland Heights. He got an apartment with his childhood friend Pete Harpen, who went to the University of Cincinnati.

Pete and George continued to hang out at the Harpen home in Mason. One day, George was there when Pete's sister, Anne, walked in to find George observing her pet cockatiel.

"That bird was crazy, he was afraid of all the activity in the house. I came in the room and George was misting the bird with a spray bottle. I said, 'What are you doing?' and he said, 'I'm simulating tropical conditions!' He was such a card."[7]

Pete and George roomed together for quite a while, though they were a mismatched pair—Pete was quite studious, Anne said. "Peter likes to say, 'I went and got my degree and George partied all night—and look where he is!'"[8]

But back then, George thought he was nowhere. He was studying TV journalism at NKU and also helped out with news reporting at his mother's cable-TV access show, but he felt he was simply hanging onto his family's coattails, wanting to do something that was completely his.[9]

"I grew up around live television. That's always what I figured I'd do. The truth is, if I was going to remain in Cincinnati, Ohio, and go into broadcasting, I was always going to be Nick Clooney's son. I'm certainly not as good as he is. That's a tough act to follow, something I was not capable of doing," he said, once he'd been in Hollywood a few years but before his big success there.[10]

In the early 1980s, when George was having those thoughts, Nick Clooney had just pulled off an incredible feat, knocking off the newscast that had been number one in Cincinnati for 22 years.

"When his station became number one, it ended a 22-year run by the city's preeminent newsman at that time. George figured, whatever I did, it wouldn't match that," said Cincinnati Enquirer TV critic John Kiesewetter.[11]

"I realized I wasn't very good at it and I realized I wasn't really bright enough or educated enough to be a journalist," Clooney said.[12] His inspiration came in the spring of 1981, when his uncle, Jose Ferrer (Aunt Rosemary's husband) and his sons, cousins Miguel and Rafi Ferrer, came to Lexington, Kentucky, to work on a movie. Miguel encouraged George to join them there, so he dropped out of Northern Kentucky University and spent three months on a sofa in Miguel's hotel room.[13]

Clooney was hired as an extra, playing a stable hand, in the movie And They're Off. The movie was never released, but for George, "this exposure to acting was love at first sight and he never looked back," his mother wrote.[14]

"He loved it," Nina said. "He invited the entire cast and crew to Easter dinner."[15]

George's lukewarm interest in broadcasting morphed into a full-blown thirst for acting. The experience on the set in Lexington "gave me the acting bug," he said.[16]

In a stroke of what has to be considered more of Clooney's luck—how often does a Hollywood production appear in Kentucky, one with relatives involved?—Clooney finally found the passion he'd been searching for. "Acting became something I really wanted to do. It was something that I would not be competing with my father in," Clooney said. "In acting, I got to be just George."[17]

He talked about acting all the time, said a friend who spent time with him in those days. "He always talked about going to California to be an actor. I thought he probably would because of his connections, his dad being in the public eye and his aunt—he was such a ham and so personable. I always thought he would do it," said old friend Kathy Penno Kramer.[18]

During the six to seven months Kramer spent time with Clooney, she remembers him spending a lot of time with his guy friends, "out and about doing stuff." She remembered many of the same things current friends say about him: he loved to play basketball, he was a practical joker, and he enjoyed making people laugh.

"When he used to come over and pick me up, he'd always bring a basketball with him because it took me forever to get ready.

"We used to go down by the river and just talk. That's what he'd talk about—what he wanted to do. His parents wanted him to finish college. He was funny, he lived in this apartment with only a bed and a director's chair—one of those canvas chairs. I knew a guy who lived near him and he said they used to have egg fights and throw raw eggs at each other in that apartment."[19]

George has acknowledged those weren't his finest days. "My dad gave me a little money to go to college, but I was a lousy student," he said. "It was the first time I'd gotten out of the house and I was hanging out with the guys all of the time. I blew all of my money pretty quickly."[20]

Derrick Davis was a student at Northern Kentucky University in the early 1980s when he used to play foosball or pool in the student center game room and run into George often.

"There were times we were late or just flat out missing class altogether," Davis wrote. "One day, George said to me, jokingly, 'Derrick! You never seem to be able to make it to class,'—as if to say 'you're never going to amount to anything if you don't start.' I said to him, 'You've got your nerve, I'm not here playing pool by myself.' His response was, 'But, Derrick, you don't understand, I'm going to be making movies some day.' It was sort of funny, because George didn't say it in a bragging way, but by the look on his face, I somewhat had to believe him. It really didn't hit me that George had made good on his promise until I was actually paying the movie attendant for tickets and saw George's face flash on the screen as Batman!"[21]

Kramer had the sense that Clooney was treading water—she wasn't sure if he was enrolled at the time at University of Cincinnati when she met him, but she was pretty sure his parents thought he was going there. "George was just kind of biding his time until he could get to Hollywood, because that's exactly what he wanted to do and he knew that's what he wanted to do," she said.[22]

The pair broke up in late 1981, but when Kramer's friend was killed in a car accident not long afterward, she called George to ask him to find the news reports through his dad. To this day, she remembers with fondness the kind way he treated her as he got her the information she needed.

In the late summer of 1982, with his cousin Miguel encouraging him, Clooney finally left for California—but not before having a fight with his parents. It was a tense time they all remember quite well.

"It was a real battle with them over leaving," he said. "They were afraid I'd be a waiter for the rest of my life."[23]

"When his father tried to convince George to stay in school by saying, 'At least with a diploma, you'll have something to fall back on,' George replied, 'If I have something to fall back on, I'll fall back,'" his mother wrote.[24]

Nick recalled, "It was the most nonsensical thing I'd ever heard in my life. I told him that his chances of succeeding were about one in 1,000." But George responded, "Pop, I'm going to do this with my life. It's what I think I will be best at."[25]

Clooney had to convince at least one other person that going to Hollywood was not some crazy boondoggle. Bill Lawrence had gotten to know George Clooney as a regular customer of his small branch of Citizens National Bank in Crestview Hills, the mall where George worked at McAlpin's. Lawrence was the manager, but when he was short a teller, he'd work the windows.

"We all knew who George was because of his dad being on TV—we'd all kind of grown up with Nick and there was no doubt whose child he was because he looked so much like his dad," said Lawrence.[26]

Whenever he came in, however, Lawrence had to calm down the 20- to 25-year-old women tellers. "They got all excited, it was almost a fight to see who was going to wait on him when he came in. Whenever I needed a spare teller, I'd get the question, 'Is it McAlpin's payday? Will I get to see George?'"

He was a very personable young man, Lawrence said. "He had no airs about him, he was just an everyday, nice kid. He'd come in and we'd get to talking—I think he was wasting a little time before going back to work, like any kid—we'd talk about school or whatever. One day he was going to be an investment banker, another day a stockbroker, then he wanted to know how to get into banking. He was just a young man trying to figure out what he was going to do."[27]

This went on over the year or year and a half that George worked at McAlpin's until the day he came in to close his account.

"I'm going to Hollywood," he told Lawrence.

"Why do you want to go to Hollywood?" Lawrence asked. When Clooney replied that he was going to become an actor, Lawrence said, "Son, come sit here."

He and Lawrence sat for a few minutes, and Lawrence asked him if he was sure he wanted to do that. He said he was getting a car from his dad and going to live with his Aunt Rosie for a year.

"Son, a whole bunch of people who go there come home broken," Lawrence said. George replied, "I'm going to give it a try."

Years later, while walking through another Cincinnati-area mall, Lawrence was with his seven-year-old son, who spotted "Batman" walking through the mall wearing jeans, gym shoes, and a black leather jacket, looking as if "he hadn't shaved in a couple of days."

Lawrence yelled, "Hey Batman!" and Clooney looked at him for a moment. Then, he said, "I know you. You're my banker." He turned to the woman he was with—a blonde woman who didn't look happy to be in Kentucky, according to Lawrence—and said, "This man told me not to go to Hollywood."[28]

Lawrence told Clooney then that he was glad he'd been wrong and that George was doing well making movies. Lawrence laughs at the memory of those long-past days.

Nick Clooney finally gave George the keys to a 1976 Monte Carlo with 200,000 miles on it to get to the West Coast, but not until he earned it. George had spent time that summer cutting tobacco on his grandfather's farm and working at an Augusta festival drawing caricatures and selling lemonade.

Loaning him money "wasn't my father's way," Clooney said. "His thing was [about] taking care of yourself. And he hated the idea [of going to Los Angeles]."[29] (Ironically, just eight months after George moved to L.A., his father took a job as anchor of L.A.'s KNBC news.)

After Clooney left for California, he came back to town for visits and always stopped at McAlpin's, Schwartz said. "If I wasn't there, he'd leave a note on my locker," she said. "I thought for sure he'd make it good in California, he had that in him." One person was sure, at least.

Loading his things into the rusty Monte Carlo in 1982, George Clooney drove more than halfway across the country (the car broke down at least once, in Tulsa) to Los Angeles and moved into his Aunt Rosemary's house.[30]

"My aunt made me get rid of it when I moved out here," George said of the car. "It was such an ugly car for living in such a nice area of Beverly Hills. She was too embarrassed."[31]

It wasn't long before he moved out of his aunt's spacious home and into the small apartment of a friend, actor Thom Mathews. Clooney lived in Mathews's walk-in closet, sleeping on a mattress on the floor.[32]

The people George met in those early years in L.A. are the people he has long considered his closest friends—the guys known as "The Boys," including Thom Mathews, Richard Kind, Ben Weiss, and Grant Heslov, whom George met in acting class in 1983.

"It's a big web of fun. Sundays, everybody comes by and everybody plays basketball, and we're all really close and really supportive of one another," he said.[33]

Weiss, now an assistant director of television shows, remembered those early days when he first met Clooney, calling him an overexcited country boy.[34]

It didn't take Clooney long to find work, though he was living on the cheap. He borrowed money for head shots and arrived for auditions on a bicycle; he also took acting classes and paid his tuition with earnings from small construction jobs.[35] Within six months of arriving in L.A., he had snagged a costarring role in the movie *The Predator*, about a man-eating bear. His character got eaten in his sleeping bag about halfway through the never-released film.

In March 1984, Clooney was selected for a part as a male prostitute in a play, *Vicious*. The production, which told the story of English punk rocker Sid Vicious, was directed by Dorothy Lyman. Clooney considered it a turning point in his early career, and his father, who saw the play a half-dozen times, agreed, noting that his son's confidence on stage had obviously grown with each performance.[36]

"That role was what really kicked things into gear for me. Producers have to see you in something before they'll hire you," Clooney said.[37]

George credited his uncle, Jose Ferrer, for helping him with the theater role. "He came to see me—it was this little Equity waiver play in downtown Los Angeles—and I thought I was brilliant in it," Clooney said. "I was crying and yelling and doing everything I thought was brilliant and then at the end of it, he's sitting there and I walk over and say, 'What did you think, Uncle Joe?' And he goes, 'I would say to you to keep the scenery out of your mouth, you don't know where it's been.' He was a great teacher for all of that!"[38]

That part led to roles in episodes of the TV shows *Riptide* and *Street Hawk*. On *Street Hawk*, a new series about a crime-fighting motorcycle, he played his first bad guy, a change Clooney relished. Along the way, some classic Clooney tales emerged, similar to the stories his childhood friends told about him and which displayed what the local papers once referred to as his knack for "being mischievous without ever getting in any real trouble." One, in which young Clooney was driving a car with a camera mounted on the hood for a scene in episode 2 of *Street Hawk*, began when his director asked him to accelerate to 60, cut the wheel, and flip the car into a U-turn. "But no one told the security lady what we were doing. Action. So I come around the corner and here comes a bus loaded with tourists. I lose control of the car and smack into a light pole. The pole falls, totals the car, and smashes the camera. I'm thinking, 'Jeez, I'm going to kill a hundred people and ruin my career in the process.' But everybody on the bus thinks it's part of the tour, and they applaud like crazy."[39]

The day after he received what he called both an "incredible check" and "an ungodly amount of bucks" from ABC for his work in *Street Hawk*, Clooney got his first regular role on a TV series, for *E/R*. CBS's

E/R, with Elliot Gould and Jason Alexander, is not to be confused with the show that later made Clooney a household name, NBC's *ER*. On this first *E/R*, Clooney played an emergency medical technician named Ace who was a sort of street kid and rock 'n' roller. It was the same sort of George-like antics, the things his coworkers and friends had always known him to do, that got him the part.

"When we wrote the part of Ace, he was supposed to be in a band called the Falcons," said *E/R* executive producer Bernie Orenstein. "So George comes in for the audition. He's mumbling his lines between bites of a hoagie. Then he pulls open his shirt, and he has some kind of fake tattoo on his chest that says, 'The Falcons.' It was totally in character. We signed him on the spot."[40]

Though George's personality, looks, and talent obviously were instrumental in the way he managed to get part after part, it didn't hurt that he had family in town who knew the ropes and could guide him. Though he'd left Cincinnati to escape his father's shadow, he wasn't above listening to California relatives-by-marriage.

"I'll tell you, having Jose Ferrer for an uncle has been a big help," the 23-year-old Clooney said at the time. "He's encouraged me the whole way. But I've had some lean times the past two years. Out here, everyone's an actor—waiters, cabbies, everybody. So it sure feels good to be working."[41]

Nick, then anchoring an L.A. newscast for KNBC, was clearly pleased with his son's ability to land a job. "I told the people at KNBC news that Wednesday night at 8:30, every TV monitor in the newsroom will be tuned to Channel 2" because *E/R* would be on.[42]

Good thing *E/R* didn't go on right before the nightly newscast on the CBS station. "That's the least he could do for his old man," Nick said.

Clooney's episodes of *E/R* went well, and in the weeks he appeared on the show, it climbed from 62nd place in the Nielsen ratings to 29th. "That's not all my doing," Clooney told the local papers. "But the timing's good, it ought to help when negotiations roll around."[43]

He was obviously picking up a lot in a short time about the business of acting and developing his own M.O. for making the most of the chances he got. "I'd rather not have a whole lot of scenes," he said. "It's better just having a few good lines. Less chance of being typecast. The idea is to make sure you don't limit yourself."[44]

Things were going even better than planned, considering it was just a week into the network pilot season in January 1985 for the following fall and he already had offers for regular roles in three series.

"It's only the fifth day of the season," he said. "I have four months to go, four months to be a little selective."[45]

Four months later, with *E/R* canceled, he signed a one-year contract with NBC for a regular role in *The Facts of Life*, a series about four boarding school girls who live with their housemother. It was produced by Embassy Television, which also produced *E/R*. Discussing his new role just days after his 24th birthday, Clooney talked about earning a regular salary.

"I'm going to have to [think about incorporating]," he said. "But it's cool, because all of a sudden I'm making money. So now I guess I'll have to grow up in a business sense, too."[46]

His financial sense was maturing—but he wasn't exactly a grown-up yet. At the same time that he was considering his financial responsibilities and gearing up for when his regular role would begin on *Facts of Life*, he could still find time on a summer's day to cruise around L.A. One time, he was observed by a hometown reporter in a white 1960 Oldsmobile with pals Mathews and Heslov. To *Cincinnati Post* reporter David Wecker, Clooney the actor still seemed—as people would continue to say for many years—"like the same old kid."[47]

"True, he now has an agent and publicity people. He's also getting into CDs and money markets and is looking seriously at land in South Carolina. But he sees the changes in more basic terms: 'I've got my own toilet, got money, got my own dartboard and my own answering machine,'" Wecker wrote.

As they drove, they got near the house Clooney had lived in for a while, his Aunt Rosemary's place, and drove past actor Jimmy Stewart's home.

"He bought the lot next door. It had this beautiful house and he tore it down because he wanted a bigger garden," Clooney said. "Pretty chi-chi, huh?"[48]

He obviously had no clue what his future would be like.

NOTES

1. Dave Larsen, "George Clooney Shoots His Mouth Off," *Dayton Daily News*, June 28, 1998, p. 1C.

2. Dotson Rader, "It's Finally about Friendship and Loyalty," *Parade*, June 7, 1998, p. 4.

3. *Cincinnati Post*, "George Clooney and the New Rat Pack," December 7, 2001, p. 1B.

4. Rader, "It's Finally about Friendship and Loyalty."

5. Margaret A. McGurk and John Kiesewetter, "Curious, Funny, Ambitious George," *Cincinnati Enquirer*, March 5, 2006, p. 1I.

6. Virginia Schwartz, phone interview with author, October 27, 2008.

7. Anne Harpen, phone interview with author, October 30, 2008.

8. Ibid.

9. Rader, "It's Finally about Friendship and Loyalty."

10. John Kiesewetter, "Clooney: Look Who's Talking Prime Time," *Cincinnati Enquirer*, July 25, 1990, p. B1.

11. John Kiesewetter, phone interview with author, October 30, 2008.

12. *Cincinnati Post*, "George Clooney and the New Rat Pack."

13. Rader, "It's Finally about Friendship and Loyalty."

14. Nina Clooney, "George Clooney," in *Encyclopedia of Northern Kentucky* (Lexington: The University Press of Kentucky, 2009).

15. McGurk and Kiesewetter, "Curious, Funny, Ambitious George."

16. David Wecker, "Nick's Son Lands Series Role," *Cincinnati Post*, December 7, 1984, p. C6.

17. John Kiesewetter, "Catch a Rising Star: George Clooney Makes Name," *Cincinnati Post*, November 13, 1985, p. D1.

18. Kathy Penno Kramer, phone interview with author, March 1, 2008.

19. Ibid.

20. Kiesewetter, "Clooney: Look Who's Talking Prime Time."

21. McGurk and Kiesewetter, "Curious, Funny, Ambitious George."

22. Kathy Penno Kramer, phone interview with author, March 1, 2008.

23. Kiesewetter, "Catch a Rising Star."

24. Clooney, "George Clooney."

25. Kiesewetter, "Catch a Rising Star."

26. Bill Lawrence, phone interview with author, October 28, 2008.

27. Ibid.

28. Ibid.

29. Kiesewetter, "Clooney: Look Who's Talking Prime Time."

30. Anne-Marie O'Neill, "Boy George—At 40, George Clooney Seems as Committed as Ever to His Buddies, Basketball, a Certain Potbellied Pig—And Bachelorhood," *People*, May 7, 2001, p. 96.

31. Kiesewetter, "Clooney: Look Who's Talking Prime Time."

32. Rader, "It's Finally about Friendship and Loyalty."

33. Lorrie Lynch, *USA Weekend*, September 26–28,1997, http://www.usa weekend.com/97_issues/970928/970928cov_clooney.html.

34. Ian Parker, "Somebody Has to Be in Control—The Effort behind George Clooney's Effortless Charm," *The New Yorker*, April 14, 2008, p. 40.

35. Chris Nashawaty, "The Last Great Movie Star," *Entertainment Weekly*, December 2, 2005, p. 44.

36. Kiesewetter, "Catch a Rising Star."

37. Wecker, "Nick's Son Lands Series Role."

38. Larsen, "George Clooney Shoots His Mouth Off."

39. David Wecker, "George Clooney Is Riding High in Television in Los Angeles," *Cincinnati Post*, January 10, 1985, p. B11.

40. Ibid.

41. Wecker, "Nick's Son Lands Series Role."

42. "Another Clooney Eyes TV Career," *Cincinnati Enquirer*, December 9, 1984, p. E18.

43. Wecker, "George Clooney Is Riding High in Television in Los Angeles."

44. Ibid.

45. Ibid.

46. David Wecker, "George Clooney Gets Facts of Life role," *Cincinnati Post*, May 22, 1985, p. B7.

47. David Wecker, "Cruisin' with George Clooney in L.A.," *Cincinnati Post*, June 19, 1985, p. B3.

48. Ibid.

Chapter 4

PILOTS, MOVIES, AND *SISTERS*

George Clooney debuted on NBC's *Facts of Life* as handyman George Burnett in the fall of 1985. At about the same time, John Kiesewetter became the TV critic for the *Cincinnati Enquirer*. His first big story was about George Clooney, local boy.

"He hit it lucky with the first E/R," said Kiesewetter. "But the next 10 years, he was just a journeyman actor. He kept himself busy—to his credit—in L.A."[1]

The headline on that November 13 story was "Catch a Rising Star." In it, Clooney described to Kiesewetter his game plan. "The plan is to do *Facts of Life* until I get my name around, so I can get the films I want to do. A feature film would be fun," he said.[2]

Clooney described how he'd auditioned for films already but said he didn't get parts such as the Judd Nelson part in *Breakfast Club* or the Rob Lowe part in *St. Elmo's Fire*. "They were the name, and they got the part," he said.

What sounded reasonable in 1985 is almost funny a quarter of a century later, when Rob Lowe is a regular on a TV series (ABC's *Brothers and Sisters*) and George Clooney is a mega-movie star/director/producer. Kiesewetter reflected on the unlikely journey of the young man he first interviewed when he himself was still a young reporter: "I've done many of those interviews over the years—there have been plenty of people from here. Nothing compares to this. I had no idea he'd be different. But I'd go to L.A. twice a year on press tours and meet various stars, and he always struck me as very grounded, down to earth—a normal Midwesterner. He didn't go all Hollywood. A lot of those people have big egos, but he never struck me as such. Until after *ER*, when he moved into a new house, I had his home phone number."[3]

The Facts of Life, which Clooney called "the cleanest-cut show" he'd ever seen, was an opportunity Clooney apparently tried to make the most of. At the time, he talked about using the scripts to hone his physical comedy skills and even getting some opportunities to stretch his creative impulses by contributing to the writing.[4] But 15 years later, Clooney laughed when thinking back to his days as George Burnett, calling his performances "the worst combination of overconfidence and bad acting you've ever seen in your life."[5]

Clooney considered *Facts* a steppingstone, and it was. In November 1985, he told Kiesewetter he hoped that, when the family show completed filming for the season, he'd have some great options for his future. Sure enough, in March, there was good news. Clooney had signed a contract with Embassy Telecommunications, which had created *Facts of Life*, to develop a comedy show pilot. Kiesewetter predicted that Clooney would have his own network series within a year.[6]

"I'm established enough with Embassy that they know I can do the job," said Clooney, almost 25 at the time. "I'm not established enough that I'm stuck in just playing one single character."[7]

Clooney was contracted to be in at least six *Facts* episodes the following fall, with an option to extend if he wasn't busy with anything else by then. Things didn't turn out exactly the way Clooney or Kiesewetter guessed they would. Instead, Clooney was briefly fired from *Facts of Life* in the fall of 1986 by the show's new producer, who accused Clooney of sabotaging the weekly run-through of the show in front of network executives.

Clooney said it hadn't happened that way at all. In his version of the story, the show's cast had planned to give a poor performance because they were so disappointed in the quality of the script, but he convinced them that was a bad idea.[8] Either way, he was eventually rehired to complete that season.

Meanwhile, Clooney did something he'd been wanting to do: he made some movies. But the movies he made in 1986 and 1987 weren't the kind he had dreamed of. First, he did a made-for-TV movie called *Combat High* and then two films, *Return to Horror High* and *Return of the Killer Tomatoes*! He continued on *Facts of Life* and guest-starred on a couple of TV shows, but it was clearly a quiet time in his career, and everyone—including his father—realized he was in a lull.

"I got a handwritten note from Nick at Channel 12 around that point in the late '80s," said Kiesewetter.[9] "He said, 'I don't mean to toot my horn for George, but he just taped *Murder, She Wrote* and *Golden Girls* episodes. Maybe you can check when they'll be on?' It was the late '80s and here was dad trying to give a little push for the son, as if maybe he might not make it and have to come back home."

But then, things took off, at least in a small way. Clooney left *Facts* and snagged a regular role as Booker Brooks, Roseanne Barr's supervisor at the plastics plant, on *Roseanne*, then the number one TV show in the country. It was a high-profile job, the most exposure he'd yet had. But after 11 episodes, he decided he'd had enough.

"He was offered a stupendous amount of money to [continue to] do *Roseanne*," Nick Clooney said. "I was thinking he could build a little nest egg and maybe acting would pay off after all. He said, 'No, I'll be in a cul-de-sac. I'll be that guy, and that's all I'll be.'"[10]

It wasn't only that. Years later, Clooney admitted he hadn't been happy working on *Roseanne*.[11] One good thing that did come out of being on *Roseanne* was that Clooney adopted someone who would become a longtime and well-known part of his family—a pig named Max. The pig was brought onto the set for an episode in which Clooney's character, the factory manager, was dealing with a mouse infestation.

"The producers wanted some little pigs," Clooney said. "One of them was Max, a very little, black, Vietnamese pig. It was so nice that, when the shooting finished, I brought it home. I thought it should have been small forever. Instead, it began to grow up and today it's a giant."[12]

There was another positive side to Clooney's time spent on—and the way he left—*Roseanne*, one that the now-savvy actor/businessman understood well. "It helped being on a hit and in a show where I played an adult for the first time. And leaving a No. 1 show—rather than being asked to leave a show—gives you the illusion of being hot."[13]

In the spring of 1989, news reports speculated that Clooney might get his own series on CBS the next fall. One possibility was a comedy western coincidentally, called *Hot Prospects*, about a man who goes west with a group of women who work in his restaurant while looking for husbands. Another was a comedy based on one of three movies, *Adventures in Babysitting*, *Coming to America*, or *Married to the Mob*. None of those shows materialized, but Clooney would eventually be cast in another "movie-to-series" transformation.

In December 1989, Clooney married Talia Balsam, daughter of actor Martin Balsam and Joyce Van Patten, whom he had met in 1984 while in the cast of the play *Vicious*. He pursued her despite the fact she was seeing someone else.[14] They dated for a year and a half, broke up (during which time Clooney dated Kelly Preston), and then found each other again, taking a Winnebago to Las Vegas to get married. They divorced three years later.

"I probably—definitely—wasn't someone who should have been married at that point," Clooney said. "I just don't feel like I gave Talia a fair shot."[15]

Clooney and Balsam lived in a Hollywood Hills home with a bulldog and a cat and the 100-pound pot-bellied Vietnamese pig named Max. Many opportunities were coming young Clooney's way, one after another. First he was cast as a guitar-playing, long-haired detective in *Sunset Beat*, a series about young undercover motorcycle cops.

Sunset Beat was widely compared to another show of the same era, *21 Jump Street*. "More young, hairy, undercover cops, more noisy chase scenes, more tough-guy banter. But in gradations of junk, *Sunset Beat* is more amusing than *Jump Street*. . . . Then, too, the cast is more adept than *Jump Street*'s hunky lunks. *Sunset Beat*'s prime stud is played by George Clooney (yes! Nephew of Rosemary "Come on-a-My House" Clooney!) As (get this) Chic Chesbro, Clooney isn't sullen; instead, he's downright hostile, which is refreshing."[16]

Meanwhile, the local Cincinnati papers trumpeted the local boy's successes with headlines such as "George Clooney Comes into His Own."[17] "It should no longer be necessary to identify George Clooney as 'son of Nick, nephew of Rosemary' . . . after eight years in the land of fruit, nuts, movies and television, the 28-year-old Clooney has established himself in Los Angeles as a hot actor who's getting plenty of opportunities to become a star."[18]

Opportunities, yes. Star? Not quite yet.

The two-hour pilot of *Sunset Beat* aired that spring as a tryout for the fall season and was canceled after two episodes. *Red Surf*, a movie in which Clooney stared as a California ex-surfer who gets involved in drug trafficking, premiered around the same time at the Houston International Film Festival. Though it looked as if things were finally going his way, he wasn't satisfied.

"The problem for me is that I really want to do films, and, with the route I'm going, by doing TV you get to do film. TV isn't the taboo it used to be. You take things a lot further on film. Everything gets taken to an extreme—there's an edge that you can't get to on TV. In L.A., if you're doing TV, it's fine. But in film, if you're making a good living in film, you're in the catbird seat."[19]

There were other reasons he wanted to be in movies, reasons that belied his young age. "Because television is more temporary than movies. Because movies are immortal."[20]

But his next step, instead of making a movie, would be to land a part in a series that began as a movie. *Baby Talk* was a take-off of the popular *Look Who's Talking* movies. He was asked to read for the part the day after *Sunset Beat* was canceled. The series was then picked up, one of many lucky circumstances that caused Clooney to feel as if he were living a charmed life.[21] Yet he continued to downplay his successes and made jokes about his checkered record.

"I'm just a jinx," he said, referring to the many movies he'd made that had never been released and the many TV series that had failed. "I'm surprised this TV series made the [ABC] schedule."[22]

The summer of 1990 was an important time for Clooney. He was newly married. He was cast on the promising *Baby Talk*—which would become a turning point in his life, if not his career. And his uncle George was dying of cancer.

Clooney spent time that summer promoting *Baby Talk*—a show that was highlighted by publicists for a fall premiere but ended up not getting on the air until March 1991. The delays were often written about, starting with stories about how, a month before the new TV season was to begin in September, star Connie Sellecca was replaced. *Baby Talk* had been described as one of the few new shows that was expected to be a hit that fall because of its high marks in an *Advertising Age* panel review. But by late August, the show had been taken off the fall schedule, and Sellecca filed a lawsuit against *Baby Talk* producer Ed. Weinberger, who had replaced her. The lawsuit alleged that Weinberger "beat up on Sellecca emotionally" and "demanded she submit unconditionally to his authority."

Clooney agreed that Sellecca had been treated unfairly and wasn't shy about speaking up about his feelings, even though Weinberger was a well-known man at that time. He'd created one of the most successful and best-loved TV shows in history—*The Mary Tyler Moore Show*—as well as other classics such as *Taxi* and *The Cosby Show*. So the young Clooney was taking something of a risk when he stood up to Weinberger. He walked off the set anyway.

"The show wasn't what we wanted it to be," Clooney said two months after Sellecca filed her lawsuit. "Connie and I and virtually everyone there were unhappy. The problem was not with Connie. She is a good lady. The problem was with Ed. Weinberger."[23]

Clooney told Weinberger one day that everyone used an expletive to describe him whenever the producer left the room.[24] The bad feelings between Weinberger and Clooney, which began when Weinberger fired Sellecca, had become worse when Weinberger fired the original set of twins who played the baby in the sitcom.

"The audience hated those first babies. We had to get cute ones. The babies didn't know they were being fired. But George blamed me," Weinberger explained.[25]

Clooney blamed Weinberger for his general attitude on the set; even though he'd been searching for jobs and this job was considered a promising one on a potentially successful series, he quit.

"Ed. and I were so adamantly against each other, we knew we'd never get along. Just because you take a job as an actor doesn't mean you have to give up your civil rights. The truth is, I didn't need the money and I didn't think it was going to be my last job," Clooney said in October 1990.[26]

His father backed up his decision, despite the risk that it posed. Integrity was more important than a paycheck, Nick said.[27]

"Nick said, 'Yes, George really pushed back hard against Ed. Wein-berger,' and, in Nick's words, 'George worried it could cost him his career as being someone who was difficult to deal with,'" said Kiesewetter.[28]

Apparently part of the courage George needed to confront Wein-berger came out of the death of his beloved Uncle George. Clooney said that the experience of being with his uncle when he died significantly changed his life, and he imagined his uncle somewhere watching him, to see how he turned out.[29] The first thing he did upon returning to L.A. after his uncle's death was to quit *Baby Talk* "because he would not toler-ate what he felt was the cruel behavior on the set toward other actors."

Co-star Julia Duffy (who had replaced Sellecca) years later remem-bered George's courage. "He absolutely was not going to stand by while people were treated badly," she said. "He certainly wasn't in any posi-tion of power at the time . . . but he didn't care. He would stand up against the big guys."[30] Clooney remembers feeling that if he had failed to act on behalf of his colleagues, he would have been responsible for the consequences. When he walked away from *Baby Talk*, he thought his career had ended; in five days, he ended up in a pilot for another show.[31]

That pilot was for *Knights of the Kitchen Table*, a CBS series created by Gary David Goldberg, who had created the hit *Family Ties*. The part was offered to him without an audition, in part apparently because Goldberg was impressed by Clooney's handling of the difficult Wein-berger.

Weeks after he'd left *Baby Talk*, Clooney talked about how he'd been interested in *Kitchen Table* for other than the usual reasons—hoping to be made a star, making a lot of money, or launching a film career.[32]

"I've never done a show just because it was a marvelous script. And that's my reason for wanting to do this. This is the best script I've ever read. Ever," he said.[33]

Perhaps that was true, or perhaps it was wishful thinking at a dif-ficult time in his career. Either way, *Knights of the Kitchen Table* didn't get anywhere. Meanwhile, *Baby Talk* finally debuted with co-star Duffy in March of 1991 to terrible reviews, even in his friendly hometown papers.

"It simply isn't funny, which is a tremendous shortcoming for a situ-ation comedy," wrote Greg Paeth.[34]

The show was about Maggie Campbell and her son, Mickey, whose thoughts are spoken by actor Tony Danza. In the early episodes, Maggie deals with a crew of contractors renovating her New York loft. "The head of the crew is Joe, played by local-boy-made-good George Clooney, who doesn't seem to be all that comfortable in a role in which his blue collar distinguishes him from Maggie and the men she finds attractive," Paeth wrote.

A few months later, Paeth concluded, "George Clooney may never find the perfect TV show for his acting talents. But he may wind up holding an unofficial world's record for completing TV pilots in a relatively short period of time."[35]

True, Clooney was working on his fifth pilot in 13 months (one, called *Rewrite for Murder*, never aired), a Lorimar Television show called *Homicide*, in which a young detective in L.A. gets recognized for killing a man believed to be a serial killer who has terrorized the city. But at least he thought this one was good. "It's got a real edge to it," Clooney said about the show, produced by David Jacobs, the man behind the classic TV hits *Knots Landing* and *Dallas*.[36]

Regardless, *Homicide* also was killed. But, coincidentally, his next pilot was titled *Bodies of Evidence*. Just before that series hit the air in the summer of 1992, the local Ohio joke was, "Clooney's now made more pilots than the Wright Brothers."[37]

The evidence Clooney had at that point was that he wasn't all that great an actor, even after years of modest success getting jobs in Hollywood. He believed his cousin Miguel Ferrer—the man who encouraged him to come to Hollywood ten years earlier—was "the best actor I know."

"My category is I'm doing television—you work where the work is. I'm not insane or stupid about what I do or how good I am. I understand my limitations. I do a good job—I'm a good actor, but not what Miguel is. I'll see something Miguel does and say I can't do that. I don't say I'll never be able to do that—I just know I can't right now.

"His category is different. He'll be sitting around getting Oscars or nominations for supporting actor in a few years," said Clooney, who fortunately never considered a career in fortune telling.[38]

Bodies of Evidence, an eight-week summer series in which Clooney costarred with Lee Horsley, finished in the top 25 each week against reruns and other summer series, then was picked up by CBS for the spring, when it hit tougher competition. Clooney had high hopes for that series.

"In the past, George Clooney has been surprisingly candid about some of the TV series he's made," wrote Greg Paeth of the *Cincinnati Post*. "He talks about the ill-fated ABC sitcom *Baby Talk* the way some people talk about 10 years on a chain gang. In another candid moment, he described the short-lived motorcycle cop series *Sunset Beat* as *The Mod Squad* meets *C.H.I.P.S.* which made it clear that *Sunset Beat* did not represent landmark television. But as his latest series, *Bodies of Evidence*, returns to CBS Tuesday night, Clooney sounds much more enthusiastic and, uncharacteristically for Clooney, a bit like a booster."[39]

"It's nice to be talking about a show I can be proud of for a change," said Clooney. "I've been on shows that I really couldn't have cared less about, but I'd really like to see this one go."[40]

Part of the boosterism Paeth noticed could have been a bit of failed-pilot fatigue. But Clooney had no idea at the time how close he was to real success, even though *Bodies of Evidence* was, not surprisingly, axed.

Clooney, as always, still had work. First, he was a guest on pal Bonnie Hunt's show, *The Building*. The premise involved Hunt as a jilted bride moving back into her old apartment building across the street from Wrigley Field in Chicago. Clooney played the man who had jilted Hunt.

"But once the cameras start rolling, *The Building* is the sitcom equivalent of the Cubs, a solid but hapless effort that won't be finishing in the first division," Paeth wrote.[41]

The series was short-lived. That same summer of 1993, Clooney joined what was considered one of TV's best dramas at the time, the very popular *Sisters* on NBC. Clooney arrived in the second episode of the season as James Falconer, a detective who was investigating the rape of Cat Margolis, played by Heather McAdam, the daughter of the character Teddy Margolis, played by Sela Ward.

Clooney was slated to be Ward's love interest, and the pair had real chemistry. Finally, his TV career was ignited. At the same time, however, his personal life was disintegrating. Clooney, who had married Talia Balsam in 1989, divorced. He had been with Talia for a long time and at his age, his peers in Kentucky were getting married. He remembers the marriage as not meeting his conception of what the relation-ship should have been. Rather than work on the marriage, he decided to walk away from it.[42]

Heather McAdam remembered the day George Clooney joined the cast of *Sisters*: "I can't say when he walked into the room I went, 'Oh, my God.' He wasn't the George Clooney he is now—there's a *thing* that comes with him now. He was another actor. He was cute and charm-ing, but a lot of actors are cute and charming. When you get to know George, you see the work ethic and that he doesn't have a big head. He's not under any assumption that he's better than anyone—and that's not typical. He's one of those people what you see is what you get. Not that I got to know him *so* well, but he's very clearly that way. You get a sense there's no deception going on or that he's not sneaky, in a business where there's a lot of that—mistrust—he's someone who isn't playing angles. Americans can see that and can respond to it."[43]

It was the third season of the show—not the easiest of situations for a new cast member to walk into. "It's daunting to come to a show where we know each other and grew up together. But he had a natural wit, he didn't have to try very hard. He's the kind of person who has a presence about them, they don't have to do anything, they just have to come into a room," McAdam observed.[44]

Working with Clooney, particularly during the first season he was there, offered a great contrast with the situation her character was in, McAdam said. "He's very, very funny and charming and made working more fun. Especially the season we worked together the most—it was a long, hard season when my character was raped and there was a trial, I'm in a coma and all that stuff. He just kept everything really light and was a joy to work with. He pulls lots of pranks, too, but beneath all that, he's a real humanitarian."[45]

McAdam, who had been working in Hollywood even longer than Clooney, understood his career ups and downs. "I knew what it was like. It requires a type of tenacity—he did a lot of series that never made it. He hadn't found that one project. I remember talking to him about it—he'd done three parts back to back and none was picked up. We were commiserating. Of course, this was just before *ER*."[46]

Heather didn't guess that George was closing in on a big break. "I never suspected. It's like that, though. There are a lot of people who are like him who don't get that one break. But he kept plugging away, he had good people around him. We identified with each other. He was like, 'We'll see.' He had no idea what was around the corner for him, he didn't know if *ER* would be picked up."[47]

Having watched Clooney on the *Sisters* set with Sela Ward, Mc-Adam remembered that he was a good actor who had found a great character. "They had great chemistry. He's sexy and had charisma—that was natural. But I think he's grown as an actor. The George Clooney back then isn't the George Clooney of today. He's refined his skills, he's older and more sophisticated. That's what you hope for—it comes from picking the right people to surround yourself with. He chose to go in the right direction to grow as an actor and was conscious of the work he chooses."[48]

That became obvious in what happened next. In August 1993, as Clooney was just starting on *Sisters*, he was considering two 1994 "star vehicles—a one-hour drama pilot and a half-hour film comedy pilot."[49] As it turned out, Clooney took neither. Though he contemplated starring in an NBC cop show designed for him, he decided against it. An offer to read for a one-line part in the 1994 movie *Guarding Tess* may have had something to do with that decision. Clooney was so insulted by the size of the role that he refused to audition.

"I decided to stop thinking of myself as a movie actor working temporarily in TV and just try to do better TV," he said. "And at that moment, everything changed."[50]

He heard about a pilot for an NBC show and lobbied to be a part of it.

"On paper, *ER* was the much smaller role in an ensemble," Clooney pal Les Moonves said. "But he read both scripts and his instinct was *ER* was better. He's very smart about material."[51]

It was the decision that changed his life.

NOTES

1. John Kiesewetter, phone interview with author, October 30, 2008.
2. John Kiesewetter, "Catch a Rising Star: George Clooney Makes Name," *Cincinnati Enquirer*, November 13, 1985, p. D1.
3. John Kiesewetter, phone interview with author, October 30, 2008.
4. Kiesewetter, "Catch a Rising Star."

5. Dana Kennedy, "George Clooney and His Stormy Career," *New York Times*, June 25, 2000, p. AR11.

6. John Kiesewetter, "Clooney Jr. in Line for Own Show," *Cincinnati Enquirer*, March 28, 1986, p. B8.

7. Ibid.

8. Kennedy, "George Clooney and His Stormy Career."

9. John Kiesewetter, phone interview with author, October 30, 2008.

10. Joel Stein, "Guess Who Came to Dinner?" *Time*, March 3, 2008, p. 46.

11. Ian Parker, "Somebody Has to Be in Control," *New Yorker*, April 14, 2008, p. 40.

12. "George Clooney: The Year That Changed My Life." *Vanity Fair* (Italy), March 2006.

13. Greg Paeth, "George Clooney Comes into His Own," *Cincinnati Post*, April 19, 1990, p. 1B.

14. Dotson Rader, "It's Finally about Friendship and Loyalty," *Parade*, June 7, 1998, p. 4.

15. Cynthia Sanz, "Sexy 911, Sexiest Man Alive 1997/George Clooney," *People*, November 17, 1997, p. 77.

16. Ken Tucker, "TV Review, Sunset Beat," *Entertainment Weekly*, May 4 1990, http://www.ew.com/ew/article/0,,317316,00.html.

17. Paeth, "George Clooney Comes into His Own."

18. Ibid.

19. Ibid.

20. Lorrie Lynch, *USA Weekend*, September 26–28,1997, http://www.usaweekend.com/97_issues/970928/970928cov_clooney.html.

21. John Kiesewetter, "Clooney: Look Who's Talking Prime Time," *Cincinnati Enquirer*, July 25, 1990, p. B1.

22. Ibid.

23. John Kiesewetter, "Clooney Bound to Land Another Hollywood Job," *Cincinnati Enquirer*, October 29, 1990, p. B4.

24. Kennedy, "George Clooney and His Stormy Career."

25. Ibid.

26. Kiesewetter, "Clooney Bound to Land Another Hollywood Job."

27. Kennedy, "George Clooney and His Stormy Career."

28. John Kiesewetter, phone interview with author, October 30, 2008.

29. Rader, "It's Finally about Friendship and Loyalty."

30. Clarissa Cruz, "By George He's Got It—The Ocean's Eleven Star Proves He's Head of the Hollywood Class," *Entertainment Weekly*, December 14, 2001, p. 10.

31. Rader, "It's Finally about Friendship and Loyalty."

32. Kiesewetter, "Clooney Bound to Land Another Hollywood Job."

33. Ibid.

34. Greg Paeth, "Baby Talk Not Worth Waiting For," *Cincinnati Post*, March 8, 1991, p. 7B.

35. Greg Paeth, "George Clooney Tries with Yet Another Pilot," *Cincinnati Post*, October 1, 1991, p. 6C.

36. Ibid.

37. Greg Paeth, "CBS Plans New Summer Series," *Cincinnati Post*, May 14, 1992, p. 5C.

38. Greg Paeth, "George Clooney's Latest Series Given New Life," *Cincinnati Post*, July 21, 1992, p. 1B.

39. Greg Paeth, "George Clooney's Series Returns to CBS," *Cincinnati Post*, March 29, 1993, p. 1B.

40. Ibid.

41. Greg Paeth, "Two New CBS Sitcoms Sink Like a Stone," *Cincinnati Post*, August 20, 1993, p. 14A.

42. Rader, "It's Finally about Friendship and Loyalty."

43. Heather McAdam, phone interview with author, October 4, 2008.

44. Ibid.

45. Ibid.

46. Ibid.

47. Ibid.

48. Ibid.

49. John Kiesewetter, "The 'Other' Clooney Is a Busy Man," *Cincinnati Enquirer*, August 19, 1993, p. D1.

50. Kennedy, "George Clooney and His Stormy Career."

51. Ibid.

Chapter 5

ER—THE RIGHT THING

The year that George Clooney's life changed began with his first earthquake, on January 17, 1994. He called his parents to tell them about it.

"Pop, Max gave me a warning," Clooney said to his father. Max was Clooney's pet pot-bellied pig. "All that stuff about animals knowing about earthquakes before they happen? It's true. Ten minutes before the shaking started, Max woke me up. He was louder than I ever heard him and I couldn't shut him up. That's when the earthquake hit and all hell broke loose."[1]

The deadly Northridge earthquake, registering 6.6 on the Richter scale, was nothing compared to how Clooney's life would be shaken up before the year was over.

Hometown reporter John Kiesewetter remembers that during those months, he'd talk with Clooney occasionally and catch up on what he'd been doing. Clooney had told Kiesewetter about the Bonnie Hunt sitcom appearance. And, in March 1994, he mentioned another series.

"He said he did this thing called *ER* and it was one of the best things he'd ever done. At the time, I didn't know he'd had to argue with John Wells to audition for it," Kiesewetter said. "He wasn't the first guy they had in mind—there was some question in Wells' mind if he could do it or if that was what Wells wanted. And at the same time, Les Moonves was running Warner Brothers and they had this cop drama—a star vehicle built around Clooney. Clooney said he'd rather be in this ensemble drama called *ER* rather than star in his own series on another network . . . It had been Moonves who had kept George busy, he put him on *Sisters* and wanted to keep him under contract until they found the right thing."[2]

No one knew what that would be, but apparently George found it on his own. That summer, the summer of 1994, was to be the summer before George Clooney's life changed forever. Two people from earlier hometowns have memories of that pre-*ER* summer.

Kathy Penno Kramer, who dated Clooney shortly before he left Ohio for Hollywood, ran into George at a bar in Cincinnati. "I was there on a date with the guy I married and in walked George. He was really cute, he said, 'Penno, give me a hug.' I introduced him to Joe and Joe says, 'Oh, you're the one who keeps getting in series that keep getting cancelled right after they start.' George said, 'Yeah, that's me—I'm getting ready to start another one.' That was *ER*. It's the last time I saw him," Kramer said.[3]

Just before or after Kramer saw Clooney in Cincinnati, he was back in L.A. and walked into a hotel lobby for an interview with Kiesewetter, who noticed—probably for the last time—that Clooney could walk around in public without attracting any attention. "Nobody noticed, nobody cared," Kiesewetter wrote. "It was two months before America met Dr. Doug Ross."[4]

"I never got famous from working," the 37-year-old Clooney told Kiesewetter that day at the Universal Hilton. "There are a bunch of people out there who do what I do—but some of them manage to get famous in one or two shows. I managed *not* to get famous. And you can always get work if you're not famous."

Of course, mere weeks after that conversation, Clooney was as famous as they get.

He had enough common sense, business sense, savvy, or whatever to see how good *ER* could be," said Kiesewetter. "He took a lesser role as opposed to the starring role for whatever cop show NBC had, then stuck to his commitment [of staying five years]."[5]

Clooney turned down the lead in the police series and "made a pest of himself lobbying network executives to cast him in *ER*."[6] The new show's producers were unimpressed with Clooney's work thus far, so Clooney had to literally beg for a part.

"George went in to John Wells and sold himself," Moonves, then president of Warner Brothers, said. "I give George a lot of credit because he saw that being one of six or seven in a great show was better than being the star of a good show."[7]

The first time Nick Clooney saw his son on *ER*—two months before the series debuted, when George brought a rough-cut tape of the two-hour pilot episode to his parents' hotel room in L.A.—he and his wife were overcome with emotion. Though the rough cut had no sound effects and no music, when it ended, they celebrated, believing it was the best pilot they'd ever seen. They were not surprised, two months later, when critics lauded the show and it became the season's surprise hit, racking up Nielsen ratings of 18.5 and ranking in the top five among all prime-time series. *Time* magazine called the show "smart," adding, "No hour on TV is more gripping."[8]

During the press tour for *ER*, Nick was in town for his work with the American Movie Channel. It only took three questions for someone to ask Nick about George. Nick said at the time, "I used to be Rosemary's brother; now I'm George's dad."[9]

Once he got the role as Dr. Doug Ross, the charming alcoholic pediatrician, Clooney began the first of many months of working harder than he'd ever worked before. The first fall shows were hectic because he was also still working on *Sisters*, where eventually he would be killed off. "I could do it because they're both made on the same lot at Warner Brothers," Clooney said. "For a few weeks there, I was riding a bicycle between the two sets."[10]

Asked whether he ever got the two roles of doctor and detective confused, he replied, "Where there was a little confusion was in wardrobe, where I'd occasionally be wearing the wrong thing," Clooney said with a chuckle. "But, once you're on the set and they tell you to jump in bed and do a love scene with Sela [Ward], you know what to do. You're not confused. No way are you going to take her heart rate or stick a thermometer in her mouth. When you do a love scene with Sela, you know what to do."[11]

Over at *ER*, George also knew what to do. When he wasn't creating the beloved character of Doug Ross—who, as it turned out, had several traits like those of George Clooney—he was repaying favors to his relatives. Miguel Ferrer, George's cousin, friend, and mentor, had an *ER* cameo as a patient who received a death sentence on one episode. On another, Rosemary Clooney guest-starred.

"George recommended that his Aunt Rosemary be given a small but high-impact part in episode two. It involved a disoriented patient. As soon as the director called and offered the part, Rosemary phoned us. She was exhilarated and terrified. She read the script and knew it would be the most challenging acting role he had ever undertaken. It was," wrote Nick.[12]

George told his father after shooting, "Pop, she was terrific. Everybody was impressed. Wait until you see the crying scene. It was an amazing performance."[13]

When television viewers finally got to see *ER*, they were facing a bit of a strange confluence—two brand-new hospital dramas debuted on two networks, not only scheduled for the same time, 10 P.M. on Thursdays, but also set in the same city: Chicago. Television columns at the time played up the head-to-head battle of the hospitals, generally assuming that one of the two would emerge to take the "medical drama" place vacated by the beloved *St. Elsewhere*, which had ended in 1988. CBS's show, *Chicago Hope*, starred Mandy Patinkin and Adam Arkin and had been created by *L.A. Law* writer David E. Kelley, while NBC's *ER* touted Anthony Edwards, Sherry Stringfield, and George Clooney and was the creation of *Jurassic Park* author Michael Crichton.

Though similar in the fact they both were set in hospitals, the shows had some significant differences. *Chicago Hope* was set in fancier surroundings and its doctors were at the top of their fields, whereas *ER* was set in Chicago's public hospital, called County General but assumed to be based on Chicago's Cook County Hospital, in the much rougher emergency room.

"Neither series is a graduate of the *Marcus Welby* school of medicine. The doctors are flawed, not godly, and the staff rather than patients are the focus. The doctor-patient relationship also differs from the intimate, warm-and-fuzzy one usually drawn on TV. Both programs went for known actors but shunned glamour casting, or as Wells put it, 'young doctors in love.'"[14]

Once the programs had aired, critics lined up on either side, praising one or the other and, occasionally, both. "Inevitably, some critics didn't get it," wrote Nick Clooney. "Some thought, for instance, that *Chicago Hope*, an excellent program in the traditional soap-opera mode, was better. If anyone can call a subjective opinion wrong, those critics were astoundingly wrong. Network TV was being declared dead. In 1994, *ER* came along with ratings numbers that surpassed those of the 'golden era.'"[15]

ER was a true phenomenon, shooting to the top of the ratings immediately and staying there, with 45 million viewers a week.

As Nick Clooney hinted in his column, George tweaked the original character of Dr. Ross a bit to further endear him to the public. Ross was intended originally to be a bit of a creep, at least as far as women were concerned. Instead, thanks to Clooney's influence and suggestions, Dr. Doug Ross turned into a charmingly flawed flirt whose relationship with Nurse Hathaway was a love story to which countless women were drawn.[16]

When *ER*'s first season ended, it took only a couple of more months until the cast got more than popular recognition: Emmy nominations for all six leading members of the cast, three for lead actor/actress and three for best supporting actor. Clooney was nominated as best leading actor in a dramatic series. Even more amazing was that Rosemary Clooney was nominated for best actress in a guest role. A friend of Nick's told him on the phone, and it began another milestone day for the Clooney family. "If I hadn't been sitting down, I would have had to sit down. George and Rosemary. Both nominated as the best American television had to offer in a great television year. Wow," Nick wrote.[17]

Next thing he knew, George was on the phone, calling with the news, "sounding like a little boy again, happy that his baseball team pulled one out." Nick Clooney then called his sister, unconcerned about waking her up at 7 A.M., like a typical younger brother, and realizing she might not have heard about her nomination. In fact, she hadn't heard about George's nomination or her own.

"All right, George!" Rosemary said to Nick. Then, he asked her, "Did you hear about you?"

"For the second time that morning, there was a long silence. Then, 'What about me?' 'You were nominated, too.' 'I don't care what happens now. They actually nominated me!' Like George, she sounded like a teenager." Nick wrote. "George, the 13-year overnight success. Talent, hard work, tough choices and a modicum of good luck had landed him in the middle of a great show. He knows some fine actors never get a chance to be part of a great project. Perhaps a lesson he can teach us is never to give up on your dream, no matter who tries to discourage you. Including your father."[18]

The only *ER* nominee who won was Juliana Margulies, who played Nurse Hathaway. Ironically, the lead actor on *Chicago Hope*, Mandy Patinkin, won in the best actor category—but, as always, Clooney took a bump in his long road to stardom with a smile. "The day after the Emmys, I called him at home and he answered the phone," said Kiesewetter. "The first words out of his mouth as he picked up were, very glibly, 'Losers' Headquarters!'"[19]

That was the last of this sort of phone call that Kiesewetter had, after writing about Clooney for many more years than most journalists. He, like the others, splits Clooney's life into before and after *ER*. Before *ER*, Kiesewetter had Clooney's home phone number and called him whenever he had questions for a column. But that September, Clooney bought a new house (with a new phone number) and acquired a publicist.

"After the Emmys, he moved, and he was starting to film *From Dusk till Dawn*. After that, he had a publicity firm, and sometime after that if you wanted to get a quick phoner with George, you were referred to Stan Rosenfield's office," according to Kiesewetter. "The woman at the office asked, 'Does he know who you are?' I'd say yes, then she'd ask me to send clips to refresh his memory. I even did that. This iron wall was put up. But, when I run into him at press tour events, he'll see me, wave, and make sure he takes 10 to 15 minutes—he always reserves time for me. He knows who I am, I've been covering him for more than 20 years."[20]

Clooney dubbed the eight-bedroom Hollywood Hills house "Casa de Clooney."[21] Formerly Clark Gable's hunting lodge, the estate has basketball and tennis courts, a guesthouse, a swimming pool, a screening room, and multiple wet bars. It cost $1.1 million.

"At the time, I was real worried about making the payments. But I paid it off when I got *Batman*. So if worse comes to worst, I've still got the house," Clooney said.[22]

At various times, the house has been home to several of Clooney's "boys," including Matt Adler, who moved in for two years after his marriage broke up in 1995.

During the fall of 1994, you couldn't pass a newsstand or grocery checkout without seeing the cast of *ER* on the covers of various magazines. If, earlier, Clooney had been making good money not being famous, he was making great money becoming a household word after *ER* debuted. He visited New York with his friend Ben Weiss during that period and noticed that strangers were noticing him.[23] The *Cincinnati Post*, in February 1995, called him "one of the hottest stars on TV." Proof of his new status included covers for *TV Guide* and *GQ*, a guest spot on NBC's *Friends*, and a spot guest hosting *Saturday Night Live*.

ER had recorded a high of 24.3 rating—that is, 24.3 percent of homes with TVs were watching *ER* when it was on—and a 40 share, meaning that 40 percent of the TVs being used at that time were tuned in to *ER*. No regularly scheduled entertainment series had reached that level since *Cosby* and *Cheers* in November 1989.[24]

In May 1995, Clooney was named one of *People's* "50 Most Beautiful People" in the world. Clooney's George-like response? "I always kind of got by on personality and jokes."[25]

After several "best pilots ever," he had finally found one that hit, and the joy was obvious when he discussed the quickly classic part of the womanizing pediatric resident Doug Ross.

"There's nothing about Doug that I dislike," Clooney said. "I like that he has flaws. He has a big drinking problem, but we don't preach to anyone about it. We just show what happens. We see him try to function. And the truth is that, so far, he can function, but whenever he's off work he drinks. Down the line a bit, we may have it impair him."[26]

The gritty reality of the show came from writer Michael Crichton, who was a medical resident himself years before writing *Jurassic Park*. He shared the executive producer title with an icon: Steven Spielberg.

"Michael really wants a fast pace, moving from plot line to plot line incredibly fast, the way things can actually happen in emergency rooms," Clooney said.[27]

The show's frenetic pace was unlike anything that had been seen on TV before, and it became a trademark of the popular show. The pace, ironically, paralleled the pace of Clooney's life, which had picked up exponentially. His father juxtaposed his son's present and past in a column that appeared one year after *ER* began.

"George was at the airport. He had a layover and would come down to spend the night. He had been interviewed for MTV in New York. From MTV in New York to Heritage Days in Augusta is a culture shock. George negotiated it with aplomb."[28]

Nick wrote, "We walked down Riverside Drive to look at the craft booths. George got almost two blocks before the small knot of people around him grew to a crowd. He signed hats, arms, dinner napkins, books, pictures, boy boats. I quietly suggested a small booth—nothing extravagant—and five dollars a signature. We could split it. With what I thought was ill grace, George asked why he should split it with me. I reminded him that half of his name was mine first. He was not moved and continued to sign whatever was handed to him, gratis."[29]

The films George had been in before *ER* were either never released or forgettable. But, as his mother wrote, "His portrayal of Dr. Ross on television brought him to the attention of major movie producers and directors. Never one to shrink from an opportunity or his responsibility, George lived up to his five-year contract with Warner Brothers for *ER*, while, with their help in scheduling, he also made six movies. Half of them were filmed during summer hiatus of *ER*, and the others during regular tapings of the successful hospital drama. George was Dr. Doug Ross in scrubs in the mornings; then in the afternoons, he would jump on his bicycle and pedal across the Warner productions lot to various sound stages."[30]

Even as George began that crazy schedule, he found time to return home when he could or when he was asked to appear at an event. At one such event, the Kidney Foundation honored the Clooney family in Cincinnati in November 1995. It marked perhaps the first time that George Clooney appeared at home and was the center of attention, even though his local-hero father and nationally known aunt were in the Music Hall that evening.

"Even people who are normally reserved and seldom easily impressed swooned in George's handsome presence. Mothers were climbing over their daughters to get his autograph. Some of the city's most prominent leaders were in front of cameras, jockeying for position at his side," wrote Mary Jo Dilonardo.[31]

Clooney drank it all in and loved every moment of it. "People in other cities don't understand this, but I grew up in a microcosm of this, in Cincinnati where my father was, like, Johnny Carson. My father was huge. And so, to be a kind of extension of that—to get even more attention than my father got—it's fun. It's fun because we're a close family and we all enjoy it," Clooney said.[32]

Many, including George Clooney, have credited his quite-familiar-with-fame—and its ups and downs—upbringing with helping him deal with the craziness that came with sudden and extreme national attention. "I was pretty much groomed to be very successful because our family, Rosemary was as successful as she could be in 1950, then not successful at all. She didn't become a worse singer along the way. Things change. The rules change. And, it affected her very badly. She didn't handle it well for a while because she didn't have anybody ahead of her.

"I get the advantage of watching that and saying, 'OK, now things are going very well for me, things will not go very well for me at some point and I have to understand that I'm not as good as they say I am right now, and I won't be as bad as people say I am when things are not going well. That's my advantage of having Rosemary go first."[33]

So, while he drank in the adoration at the Kidney Foundation gala in Cincinnati, so busy that he never got anything to eat and had to go out afterward for some food, this item appeared in the local newspaper: "Tidbits from the recent George sighting: he calls his dad 'Pop' and 'The Gray Ghost.' He drank a vodka-and-cranberry-juice concoction. He wore a dark-gray suit with a peach-and-yellow flowered tie. He cocks his head and smiles that little half-smile just like he does on *ER*. He's righthanded. During dinner, he sat with his arm around his grandma, Dica Warren, Nina Clooney's mom. George is a big hugger. Besides hugging all the other Clooneys, he hugged [local personalities] Erich Kunzel and Bob Braun."[34]

So there it was—from not-famous working actor to so famous that the media reported what he drank, what he wore, and whom he hugged. All this before he even became a movie star.

NOTES

1. Nick Clooney, "Potbellied Pig Predicts Quake," *Cincinnati Post*, January 19, 1994, p. B1.

2. John Kiesewetter, interview with author.

3. Kathy Penno Kramer, interview with author.

4. John Kiesewetter, "Five Years on 'ER' Turned Struggling Sitcom Actor into Charismatic Star," *Cincinnati Enquirer*, February 18, 1999, p. 1C.

5. Kiesewetter, Interview with author.

6. Margaret A. McGurk and John Kiesewetter, "Curious, Funny, Ambitious George," *Cincinnati Enquirer*, March 5, 2006, p. 1I.

7. Kiesewetter, "Five Years on 'ER' Turned Struggling Sitcom Actor into Charismatic Star."

8. Richard Zoglin, "The Best Television of 1994," *Time*, December 26, 1994, p. 137.

9. John Kiesewetter, interview with author.

10. Thomas D. Elias, "George Clooney Made it on His Own," Scripps Howard News Service, October 18, 1994, p. B5.

11. Ibid.

12. Nick Clooney, "Rosemary Shines on George's Show," *Cincinnati Post*, August 26, 1994, p. 1B.

13. Ibid.

14. "TV Hospital Dramas in Head-to-Head Battle," *Cincinnati Post*, September 7, 1994, p. 5B.

15. Nick Clooney, "Dr. Ross, You're Leaving in Style," *Cincinnati Post*, February 19, 1999, p. 1B.

16. Ian Parker, "Somebody Has to Be in Control," *New Yorker*, April 14, 2008, www.newyorker.com/reporting/2008/04/14/080414fa_fact_parker?currentPage=all.

17. Nick Clooney, "Emmy Hopefuls Prove: Dream On," *Cincinnati Post*, July 21, 1995, p. B1.

18. Ibid.

19. John Kiesewetter, interview with author.

20. John Kiesewetter, interview with author.

21. Anne-Marie O'Neill, "Boy George—At 40, George Clooney Seems as Committed as Ever to His Buddies, basketball, a Certain Potbellied Pig—And Bachelorhood," *People*, May 7, 2001, p. 96.

22. Chris Mashawaty, "The Last Great Movie Star," *Entertainment Weekly*, December 2005, p. 44.

23. Parker, "Somebody Has to Be in Control."

24. "Clooneymania Is Rampant," *Cincinnati Post,* February 28, 1995, p. 4B.

25. "The 50 Most Beautiful People in the World," *People,* May 8, 1995, p. 70.

26. Elias, "George Clooney Made it on His Own."

27. Ibid.

28. Nick Clooney, "Our Wild Week in Little Augusta," *Cincinnati Post,* September 11, 1995, p. B1.

29. Ibid.

30. Nina Clooney, "George Clooney," in *Encyclopedia of Northern Kentucky* (Lexington: The University Press of Kentucky, 2009).

31. Mary Jo DiLonardo, "Reflections on an Evening with a Certain Clooney," *Cincinnati Post,* November 15, 1995, p. 1C.

32. Craig Kopp, "VIP Clooney's Perspective Down to Earth," *Cincinnati Post,* January 18, 1996, Perspective Extra 3.

33. Ibid.

34. DiLonardo, "Reflections on an Evening with a Certain Clooney."

Chapter 6

A MOVIE STAR

Then he became a movie star.

It was not a foregone conclusion. Many, many big TV stars have been unable to transfer their appeal from the small screen to the big one. Some observers figured it would be no different for Clooney, who had made a few awful movies already. Even his father wasn't sure it would happen.

"It's hard to fathom now, but [Nick] Clooney had doubts that George, his Oscar-winning son, would be able to convert his *ER* TV fame into box office success . . . after a decade in Hollywood with minimal star recognition," Kiesewetter wrote.[1]

"Some people fill up a big screen and some people don't—there's no way to know until you see it," Nick said.

When *From Dusk till Dawn* opened, in January 1996, Nick and Nina Clooney slipped into the back of the Maysville theater and held their breath.

"Nina and I were very nervous. Our palms were sweating," Clooney said. "As soon as he came on the screen, we both exhaled for the first time—because it was obvious that he filled up the screen. And I looked up and said, 'He's home free. Now it's in the lap of the gods as far as the material is concerned. He'll fill up the screen.'"[2]

Nick's opinion wasn't universal. Critics and the public were either confused by and/or appalled by this particular movie, billed as a "contemporary gangster vampire Western." George's performance was given somewhat better reviews, but many critics weren't convinced that Clooney would someday "fill up the screen" and be a star.

"Lucky for Clooney that he holds his own against this onslaught of tacky silliness. When he's on the screen, he owns it. And I'm pretty sure folks looking at him for future projects will see that attribute and ignore the goofiness," wrote Craig Kopp.[3]

"And George Clooney, whose previous feature film credits include *Return of the Killer Tomatoes*, goes from television stardom in *ER* to another try at leading-man stature on the big screen. Not many television actors make the transition easily, but not many look this much like Cary Grant," noted Janet Maslin of the *New York Times*.[4]

And at least one not-so-rave, from Andy Seller of *USA Today*: "George Clooney makes a decent cardboard B-movie hero, but he better keep his day job."[5]

Some observers understood that Clooney perhaps made odd choices of movies and parts because he'd learned from experience not to go for the quick fix but to aim instead for the long haul. Why play a homicidal robber who battles a swarm of Mexican vampires? Such an out-there role was perfect, director Robert Rodriguez said, because it was either that or take the "fourth banana" parts he was being offered by studio executives who didn't realize how well-known Clooney was becoming on TV.[6]

Rodriguez, who with *Dusk* partner Quentin Tarantino made up the two hottest writer-director team in Hollywood at that time, said he wasn't surprised the film was given lukewarm reviews and had figured that into his choice of Clooney for the part.

"It's a no-risk situation [for Clooney]," he explained at the time. "It's such a bizarre movie, and it's such a far left turn from what he's doing—even if he were to fail at it, or I made a bad movie, he couldn't take any heat from it. But we both secretly made a pact that we were going to work harder than anyone would expect us to, and he did. He's amazing in it, I think he's really great and shows that he's a star. To play that kind of dark character and to be that likeable—that's not an easy feat."[7]

Not only was this a difficult task, but it would set the tone for many future Clooney movies in which he played dark parts, parts that weren't an obvious fit for him. Clooney deliberately chose the movie even before he read the script, he said, for the chance to work with and learn from professionals like Rodriguez and Tarantino.

"And then you read the script and go, 'This is wild.' The only chance you're taking is being able to hold up your end with the talent that you're talking about. That's the only risk."[8]

Well, there was another risk—to his health and safety, according to ER co-star Noah Wyle, who watched Clooney keep his commitment to ER by working nearly 24/7 shooting both the TV show and From Dusk till Dawn—during which time Clooney worked sometimes until 2 A.M. on the film, only to report to the ER set at 6:15 A.M.

"I thought if George could do it, I could," said Wyle, who made a TNT movie while working on ER. "But it nearly killed me. George has more stamina than anyone I've ever met. He sleeps two or three hours a night, plus he plays basketball eight or nine hours a day."[9]

Even before Dusk premiered, Clooney was juggling more movie offers. Word was he was going to make The Green Hornet during ER's spring hiatus of 1996, but Steven Spielberg, who produced ER, snatched him away to star in The Peacemaker, the first movie under Spielberg's new DreamWorks SKG banner. Clooney still hoped to be able to star in The Green Hornet, thinking perhaps that production would wait for him. It did not.[10] So, in December 1995, Clooney, whose previous movies had been forgettable flops, had two producers fighting over him for their projects.

In January 1996, From Dusk till Dawn premiered, his first "real" movie. In February, he was set to begin filming One Fine Day with Michelle Pfeiffer. At the same time, Warren Littlefield, the president of NBC Entertainment, announced that Clooney had sealed an exclusive agreement with NBC to create and produce TV series and made-for-TV movies.

"We benefit greatly by what George does as an actor and we've got a lot of confidence that there is an equally talented producer in him, too," Littlefield said.[11] Reports said the projects would be produced by Clooney's own production company, in association with NBC Studios, but he would not star in them.

"I've been talking to NBC for several months about some specific projects I thought would be great television," Clooney said, then added, with his typical humor, "I won't be writing them, so we've got a shot."[12]

Before February ended, Clooney's star rose still higher. He was offered $25 million to take over the starring role in *Batman & Robin* and to star in two additional Warner Brothers films. It was a long way from two years earlier, when Clooney was under contract to Warner Brothers TV for $300,000 a year as a guest on *Sisters*. The blockbuster deal put Clooney into Warner's number one TV franchise as well as its number one feature-film franchise, but, characteristically, Clooney downplayed it all.

"I think it's easier to be the third Batman than it is the second," Clooney said. "Now we've kind of established that this guy can be replaced."[13]

Speculation was rampant on how Clooney would fit in all the filming—starring on *ER* while filming both *The Peacemaker* and *Batman & Robin*. As it happened, it took grueling seven-day workweeks for a year.

In December, at the end of a year in which Clooney did little but work, *One Fine Day* opened. The romantic comedy, in which Clooney played a divorced father trying to improve his parenting skills, was more of an obvious vehicle for Clooney's charm and good looks. Reviews were mostly glowing, for Clooney if not the unsurprising movie: "*One Fine Day* erases any doubt that George Clooney could make the leap from the operating rooms of *ER* to stardom in film. He has it all: a slick, sardonic manner; calm assurance; commanding presence; great looks; and, most importantly, a distinctive voice," said the Associated Press.[14]

"The boyish bachelor Clooney is on his way to parlaying his burst of fame into a flourishing film career," said the *Milwaukee Journal-Sentinel*.[15]

After noting that Clooney played "a big kid who enjoys clowning around," *New York* Times *reviewer* Janet Maslin noted, "The film goes to needless lengths to let some of its minor characters coo admiringly about Mr. Clooney. But he's such a natural as a movie star that he hardly needs false flattery."[16]

Legendary critic Roger Ebert apparently was not quite yet sold on Clooney as movie star. "Pfeiffer looks, acts and sounds wonderful throughout all of this, and George Clooney is perfectly serviceable as a romantic lead, sort of a Mel Gibson lite. I liked them. I wanted them to get together. I wanted them to live happily ever after. The sooner the better."[17]

Clooney later defended *One Fine Day*, which came and went with little attention, noting that it was meant to be "just a little film. Then they decided to release it in the middle of the Christmas rush, against all those big films. It was the wrong time."[18]

Though the movie was hardly a scintillating blockbuster, the bigger news from the set was a bet placed by Michelle Pfeiffer regarding her costar. Observing Clooney with the children on the set, Pfeiffer commented on what a great dad Clooney would be someday. He told her that fatherhood would not ever be in his future. Then he put his money where his mouth was: he bet Pfeiffer $10,000 that he wouldn't have children within the next five years.

"She doesn't understand, I give those kids [on the set] back to their parents and they go home," Clooney said.[19]

It was not the first time, and would not be the last time, the subject arose. In a 1995 interview with Barbara Walters, Clooney swore that he had no intention of remarrying or becoming a father. "I think he means it," said Clooney's father, who years earlier had brought his kids to the office and personal appearances. "If George had kids now, they would never see him."[20]

"I don't have any interest in [having kids]," Clooney said a few years later. "I just don't think that it's something you can do casually."[21]

Perhaps it was, as Clooney's friend Matt Adler suggested, that Clooney didn't want to have children he couldn't see more than half the year because he wouldn't be able to take his children to work on movie sets the way his father had taken his to his TV shows. Or perhaps it was that he didn't want to subject children to the same kind of drag-about childhood he had had. Either way, as Adler put it, "he's just not going to father someone he can't be a father to."[22]

Five years later, Clooney won the bet with Pfeiffer, but he returned her check, betting double or nothing he wouldn't have any kids by the age of 50.

Meanwhile, those betting on his performance as Batman weren't as shrewd gamblers as Clooney. The film, which premiered in June 1997, was universally panned and became something of a running joke footnote in Clooney's career.

"George Clooney is the big zero of the film," said Mick LaSalle of the *San Francisco Chronicle*. "Beyond the sheer bad luck of looking 20 years older in his Bat mask, Clooney makes a smug, complacent, one-dimensional Caped Crusader."[23]

Roger Ebert was kinder.

"Watching it, I realized why it makes absolutely no difference who plays Batman: There's nobody at home. The character is the ultimate Suit. I've always suspected they cast movie Batmans by their chins, which is all you see when the Bat costume is being worn, and Clooney has the best chin yet. But like Michael Keaton and Val Kilmer, he brings nothing much to the role because there's nothing much there."[24]

Variety blamed the scripts, as well. "None of the series' screenwriters has ever gotten a handle on how to make the character as interesting as those around him and Clooney is unable to compensate onscreen for the lack of dimension on paper. It is indicative of the ongoing flaw in the Batman franchise that the changes in leading men have so little impact on the films' popularity or effectiveness," wrote Todd McCarthy.[25]

Reviews notwithstanding, the premiere of *Batman & Robin* was a seminal event in Clooney's life and in his career. Though this was a big-time Hollywood moment for the one-time TV-pilot dropout, Clooney didn't ask a bunch of newly friendly bigwigs to sit in his row at Westwood's Village Theater; he invited family and the people who had befriended him when he was living in a closet. His father was proud of the choices his son made.

"They were all familiar faces as I looked down the row. Not many were well known to the general public," Nick wrote. "These are friends of my son, George Clooney. He has known some for the entire 15 years he has been in Southern California. He has known them all since long before the incredible success of *ER* lifted him to a rarified celebrity status and launched his film career."[26]

A few weeks earlier, Nick and his wife, Nina, had been going through old family photos, and they happened onto a photo of five-year-old George wearing his Christmas present—a Batman outfit, "complete with cowl, ears, cape and symbol on his chest." "When George appeared on the screen, 40 feet tall, in an expensively updated version of his 1966 outfit, Nina and I looked at each other and smiled."[27]

The smiles multiplied the following week when *Batman & Robin* premiered in Augusta. The *Cincinnati Post* sent Michael D. Clark to Augusta to document the pride his hometown felt in its very own big-screen Batman: "When the projector lights kick on today in thousands of movie theaters around the country, it'll be Augusta's George Clooney on the big screen. But many of the town's 1,400 residents say it's what you can't see that makes Clooney a special kind of superstar. . . . Descriptions most often used by those who remember the young Clooney invariably range from 'nice' to 'considerate,' with a sprinkling of 'jokester' thrown in. Without prompting, longtime residents will tell you that not only was Clooney a good kid who made good, but that they never heard anything bad about him, either."[28] (Other than bad reviews, of course.)

The excitement of *Batman* had hardly worn off when Clooney pulled off another big event: star of the first film, *The Peacemaker*, from the new mega-studio Dreamworks SKG, created by icons Steven Spielberg, Jeffrey Katzenberg, and David Geffen.

"No pressure there. No. No pressure. I figure once you've done *Batman*, you can do anything," joked Clooney. Then, more seriously, he added, "You know, the thing was, you don't think about that. When you're an actor, most of the time it's 'Hey, I got a job.' It's not the pressure or anything else. Mostly it's just getting the job and going to work."[29]

Clooney brought up *Batman* in that interview himself, much to the appreciation of the entertainment press corps, who then didn't have to bring it up themselves—which they'd rather not, since they almost universally enjoyed talking with the very human George Clooney.[30]

Clooney routinely laughed off the "failure" of *Batman & Robin*, noting that it earned $105 million in the United States and $220 million worldwide. Clooney's self-deprecating sense of humor about that film helped the whole subject go away.

"I'm trying to be really honest about it because if you call it like it is, you survive a lot easier," Clooney said. "You take some of the club out of their hands by being straightforward and the truth is, the movie didn't work. Now, if I'm going to say that, I have to take some of the responsibility."[31]

It didn't hurt that *The Peacemaker*—with Clooney and Nicole Kidman as Americans tracking down stolen nuclear warheads—came out soon after *Batman & Robin* and got better reviews in general, though it was no runaway hit. Still, the film cost approximately $50 million to make and earned $120 million. "It made money," said Clooney. "But not as much as the industry hoped."

One of the more positive reviews came from Kenneth Turan of the *L.A. Times*: "Both Kidman and Clooney give dependable, movie-star performances in these James Bond-ish roles and though Clooney is the same dark-eyed smiling rogue he's played in just about all his feature roles, it's a characterization that is effective."[32]

The dark eyes, the smile, and the roguishness were effective elsewhere, too—in the real world. Shortly after *The Peacemaker* left theaters, Clooney was named "Sexiest Man Alive" by *People*. His youthful troubles talking to women were long behind him.

"Call it the Clooney maneuver. It's that little head tilt he does when his chin dips down and his eyes drop to the floor. Then, wham! Those eyes are back, full of mischief and magic, atop a sly half grin that all but announces, 'Yep, I'm trouble, but you love me anyway,'" *People*'s cover story began.[33]

"And do we ever. Whether he's playing doctor in the ER, battling supervillains in *Batman & Robin* or chasing down stolen nukes in *The Peacemaker*, George Clooney has jump-started more hearts than a whole fleet of crash carts and defibrillators. 'It's very hard to look into those eyes and not be completely intoxicated,' says *Peacemaker* director Mimi Leder. Then, 'when he turns on that charm, ooooh, watch out!' says *ER* costar Yvette Freeman, who plays nurse Haleh Adams to Clooney's Dr. Doug Ross. 'George can work it when he wants to.' But Clooney is no mere boy toy—if for no other reason than, at 36, he's no mere boy. 'He doesn't look like a Ken doll,' says Ellen Crawford (Nurse Lydia Wright). 'He has those nice little crinkles around his eyes; there's an interest to his face.' And a depth to his appeal. Beyond the Batsuit bod are smarts, sensitivity, a wicked sense of humor and what his *One Fine Day* producer Lynda Obst calls 'a real visceral masculinity. The force of his attractiveness is not just his chiseled, classic good looks,' says Obst, who dubbed the actor Swooney Clooney during shooting. 'There's something that women call being a real guy. It's hard to describe, but we know it when we see it and he's it. He has a wonderful ability to make a woman weak at her knees.'"[34]

That might have helped get over those bad *Batman* reviews. And then, six months later, what he'd arguably been waiting for all of the 16 years since he moved to Hollywood in 1982 finally happened. George Clooney made a hit movie—and none too soon.

"Clooney, more than anyone, knew that he needed a hit," said the *Dayton Daily News*.[35]

So he listened to his instincts, which were always good and getting better all the time, and chose the right project. *Out of Sight*, a love story/thriller, wasn't a good opportunity or a lucky break but a script he read—after months of reading and rejecting more bad scripts than he could believe were out there. He cheered when he found it and then set about getting the job.[36]

"This is the best role I've had. I'm coming off of *Batman & Robin*, and that's a frustrating year of your life. It was hard work and I was doing the [TV] show at the same time and it was disappointing. Not just as a box-office disappointment—as a film it was disappointing, and I have to share some of the blame for that. . . . I needed to do something I really liked, and I read projects for seven, eight, nine months before I did this. I held out and waited—and I'm glad I did because this is a movie I love."[37]

Thrilled to snag the leading role opposite Jennifer Lopez in the adaptation of Elmore Leonard's novel, Clooney then found out he'd be spending five weeks in the upper Midwest in the middle of winter. And he had thought the previous year had brought hard work! He should have known when he got there that this movie would turn out differently.

"When we knocked off for the day, we played [basket]ball at the Detroit Athletic Club, which is its own little scene," Clooney said. "It was great. I'd hang with the lowlifes all day, then shoot hoops with the captains of industry. I can honestly say that my experience in Detroit was the best, especially considering what I got out of it."[38]

There was no underestimating what he got out of it, though he tried. How important was it for Clooney's mostly-miss film career that *Out of*

Sight turn out to be a hit? Critics wrote that it was essential, but he was more casual about the dramatic pronouncements.

"At this point in my life, I've come to realize that certain things have always been true for me. Success for me has always been a long, slow process. As long as they give me another job, I'll keep showing up and I'll worry about it later. I'm going to end up on *Hollywood Squares* someday anyway."[39]

Asked whether there were times he worried it would all be over, he answered, "I might if I was just starting. But I did television that wasn't that successful for 15 years and managed to work the whole time. Yes, I'm concerned, but I still think I'm in a good place."[40]

Within days after Clooney downplayed the importance of the film, his colleagues and the press began to trumpet its hopefulness for him.

"The crime caper yarn he hopes will establish him as a major movie star," the *Record*, a Southam newspaper, in Ontario, Canada, said.[41]

In *Out of Sight* Clooney played bank robber Jack Foley who catches the attention of a federal marshal, played by Lopez. "This guy is a movie star," said director Steven Soderbergh. "He just hasn't had the material which would define him for us that way. George reminds me of Robert Redford before *Butch Cassidy*. He was an actor who was well thought of, but he wasn't a movie star."[42]

"For any actor, Jack Foley is a great role," Soderbergh continued. "But for George, this is his Butch Cassidy, the role that will finally show what he can do."[43]

"As fans of *ER* are well aware, George Clooney looks like a movie star. His only problem is finding the right role to bring him success on the big screen," wrote Stephen Schaefer of the *Boston Herald*. "That seems ready to change with Friday's arrival of *Out of Sight*."[44]

A few critics came from the opposite angle: *Out of Sight* better be great, or else.

"There are rumors that if his new film doesn't hit pretty big, his chances at being a true superstar are slim," wrote Mal Vincent.[45]

Clooney responded to that one, "I've either done OK or flopped, depending on who you talk to. Who has time to worry about it? Sooner or later they get tired of seeing you. It happens. Very few people have a career like Paul Newman—a career that lasts 40 years."[46]

Though he referred, yet again, to his solid belief that, like Aunt Rosemary, his "megastar" status would eventually end, it actually was just beginning—and the reviews for *Out of Sight* made a Newman-like career finally sound feasible. The wave of raves covered both the movie and its male star, formerly best known as a TV doctor.

"And just as one was beginning to doubt whether Clooney would make the leap from TV star to movie star, he comes up with a performance that mixes charm, edge and rage in beguiling fashion," said David Ansen of *Newsweek*.[47]

"*Out of Sight* is easily Clooney's best film performance," wrote the *Cincinnati Post*'s Craig Kopp. "He has a character to work with that fits the bad boy hunk image he built on *ER*."[48]

And it wasn't just the friendly hometown press. Critics across the country seemed downright relieved for him and happy he had finally come into his own.

"George Clooney fans can relax," wrote Philip Wuntch, film critic for the *Dallas Morning News*. "He shines in *Out of Sight*. Mr. Clooney cannot be blamed for *Batman & Robin* or *The Peacemaker*, neither of which required more than casual charm. And he definitely showed promise in *One Fine Day* opposite Michelle Pfeiffer. He fulfills that promise with *Out of Sight*, playing a role that requires both charm and substance."[49]

Marshall Fine of Gannett Suburban Newspapers wrote that this was "the movie George Clooney's been waiting for . . . a role that shows both his tough, comic edge and his more vulnerably romantic side. Here, finally, is the film that should make him a movie star."[50]

Even Roger Ebert of the *Chicago Sun-Times* finally jumped on board the Clooney bandwagon with this classic-movie high praise: "At the center of the film is the repartee between Jennifer Lopez and George Clooney, and these two have the kind of unforced fun in their scenes together that reminds you of Bogart and Bacall."[51]

Ebert gushed even more over Clooney in particular: "Clooney has never been better. A lot of actors who are handsome when young need to put on some miles before the full flavor emerges; observe how Nick Nolte, Mickey Rourke, Harrison Ford and Clint Eastwood moved from stereotypes to individuals. Here Clooney at last looks like a big screen star; the good-looking leading man from television is over with."

Wow. So what was the difference? What finally made critics and, perhaps, George himself decide that this performance was his turning point from a TV actor who dabbled in films to full-fledged movie star with a future? Some say it was the director, Steven Soderbergh. (Coincidentally—or not—Soderbergh and Clooney years later partnered in a production company.)

Soderbergh "has been credited with freeing Clooney from that tic of his, where he holds his head down and peers up into the camera," wrote Elvis Mitchell of the *Fort Worth Star-Telegram*.[52] (Good thing he didn't lose that move any sooner, seeing how it seemed to figure in his "Sexiest Man" title.)

"People see this performance of Clooney's and say, 'Gee, how did you get him to stop doing that?'" said Soderbergh. "I really didn't. He came in knowing what he had to do. I was very impressed by him. He's smart about acting. Or, rather, smart about his acting. . . . I felt this role provided George with the opportunity to do the things that he does very well, and he's not often asked to do, or allowed to do, or given the time to do. There's a gravitas to George that he hasn't got to show very much, a resigned quality to him that, in this film, I think is very compelling."[53]

Yet, in other interviews, Soderbergh didn't deny having some effect on Clooney. He admitted to stripping down what he called Clooney's mercurial approach, forcing him to be still. Dave Larsen of the *Dayton (OH) Daily News* said that Soderbergh "wiped the smirk off George Clooney's face."[54]

"'That's hard for an actor,' Soderbergh said. 'It's hard to believe that you can stand there and not do a lot and still have people want to watch you, but he can. He's compelling.' The result is Clooney's most impressive performance, in the best film of his career."[55]

Soderbergh, in effect, convinced Clooney he didn't always have to be entertaining everyone; he could just be. It was the slight tweak that made all the difference.

One footnote about the film—or perhaps the word is "chest-note." There was plenty of buzz about the movie's seduction scene, in which Clooney and Lopez perform a sort of strip poker. It was the first time Clooney had been so exposed on film.

"Look, it's always intimidating when somebody says, 'Take your shirt off onscreen,'" Clooney said. "I'm a 37-year-old guy, so I worry how that's going to look. Every single flaw is up there."[56]

On his weekly TV show, he purposely did not flaunt his chest.

"I don't do it in the show. Ever. Because on a television show like this, that's not what this show is about. I never wanted to be used as that, it's such an easy trick for the writers. And they do it, they write: 'He comes into the locker and takes his shirt off.' I always just laugh, and everyone on the crew laughs, because they know I just don't do it. It was never where I wanted to be with that guy. . . . Because I've been cast as those before, and this wasn't that. But as my involvement became more prominent [in the pilot he was in only four or five scenes] about a year into the show, it became, 'OK, let's make George this [hot hunk].' But I didn't want that. Because it's too easy then for everyone to cast you off into this category, and no one takes you seriously."[57]

In real life, however, at least one person took him seriously. In a year when everything was going right, Clooney also had a new girl-friend, Celine Balitran, a French law student and model who was one of People's "Most Beautiful People" for 1998. They met in a barn at a country home in France.

"We talked for four days because we were at a really long party. Then I followed her to a bar where she was working and basically stalked her," Clooney said.[58]

Though there were reports the couple was engaged, Clooney denied it. "I'm not going to be getting married," he said. "I don't want any kids; I've said that a million times. I can't speak for forever, I can only tell you how I feel. For Celine, that's been fine. If she changes her mind, that would be something we'd have to think about and reconsider."[59]

Two other notable events happened in that pivotal year. Clooney had a cameo role in Terence Malick's war drama The Thin Red Line and was said to be considering another film with Soderbergh, this one to be called Leatherheads, about the birth of the NFL in the 1920s. That project would be delayed for years.

But the biggest news was his announcement that the 1998–1999 television season would be his last as Dr. Doug Ross. When his original five-year contract—which he honored to the letter—ran out, he would leave the part that made him famous, saying by then that he'd have run the gamut of the role.

He first made the highly anticipated announcement on Howard Stern's radio show, after being pressed by the host. Clooney later said, "ER wasn't a stepping stone for me. It was a landing area."

Pal Brad Pitt later described Clooney's path up to that point in his career.

"I love that no one saw him coming," Pitt said. "He wallowed around for 10 years—which he'll be the first person to tell you about, and then he hit on *ER*. Even at that point, you could say, 'OK, he's defined: That's the guy on *ER*.' But from there, by his sheer will and charm and wit alone, he keeps surprising us."[60]

NOTES

1. John Kiesewetter, "Nick Clooney Waited to Exhale Until Son George Hit it Big," *Cincinnati Enquirer*, September 12, 2008, p. 6E.

2. Ibid.

3. Craig Kopp, "Critics Gentle with George," *Cincinnati Post*, January 20, 1996, p. 10A.

4. Janet Maslin, "Film Review: Enough Blood to Feed the Thirstiest Vampires," *New York Times*, January 19, 1996, np.

5. Andy Seller, "Dusk till Dawn Spares No Gory Detail," *USA Today*, January 19, 1996, p. D4.

6. Craig Kopp, "Hot Film Pair Praises Clooney," *Cincinnati Post*, January 25, 1996, Perspective Extra 7.

7. Ibid.

8. Craig Kopp, "VIP Clooney's Perspective Down to Earth," *Cincinnati Post*, January 18, 1996, Perspective Extra 3.

9. John Kiesewetter, "Five Years on 'ER' Turned Struggling Sitcom Actor into Charismatic Star," *Cincinnati Enquirer*, February 18, 1999, p. 1C.

10. "Clooney Drops 'Green Hornet,'" *Cincinnati Post*, December 12, 1995, p. 1B.

11. "Clooney Signs as Producer," *Cincinnati Post*, February 13, 1996, p. 12A.

12. Ibid.

13. Craig Kopp, "Clooney Betting Diapers Can Wait," *Cincinnati Post*, December 19, 1996, Perspective Extra 3.

14. Bob Thomas, "'One Fine Day' Mix of Comedy, Romance—Clooney Has Terrific Big-Screen Presence," *Peoria Journal-Star*, December 26, 1996, p. C4.

15. Duane Dudek, "No Longer Geeks—George Clooney and Michelle Pfeiffer Can Remember When They Felt That Way," *Milwaukee Journal-Sentinel*, December 18, 1996, p. E Cue.

16. Janet Maslin, "Meet. Fight. Fall in Love. What a Day!," *New York Times*, December 20, 1996, p. C22.

17. Roger Ebert, "'One Fine Day' Has One Predictable Plot," *Chicago Sun-Times*, December 20, 1996, Weekend Plus, p. 31.

18. Mal Vincent, "Is Superstar Status in Sight for Clooney?" *Orlando Sentinel*, June 27, 1998, p. E9.

19. Craig Kopp, "Michelle Pfeiffer Talks About Being a Mother," *Cincinnati Post*, December 19, 1996, Perspective 12.

20. Cynthia Sanz, "Sexiest Man Alive 1997/George Clooney," *People*, November 17, 1997, p. 77.

21. Herb Ritts, "Catch Him If You Can. (Actor George Clooney.)," *Vogue*, June 2000, p. 184.

22. Anne-Marie O'Neill, "Boy George—At 40, George Clooney Seems as Committed as Ever to His Buddies, Basketball, a Certain Potbellied Pig—And Bachelorhood," *People*, May 7, 2001, p. 96.

23. Mick LaSalle, "Batman Chills Out—George Clooney Can't Fill Batsuit, so Uma and Arnie Save Lightweight Sequel," *San Francisco Chronicle*, June 20, 1997, p. C1.

24. Roger Ebert, "Suit of Armor—Real 'Batman' Shielded by Gadgets, Special FX," *Chicago Sun-Times*, June 20, 1997, Weekend Plus, p. 31.

25. Todd McCarthy, "Batman and Robin," *Variety*, June 16, 1997, p. 34.

26. Nick Clooney, " 'Batman' Makes Parents Proud," *Cincinnati Post*, June 16, 1997, p. 1B.

27. Ibid.

28. Michael D. Clark, "Augusta Beams for Batman," *Cincinnati Post*, June 20, 1997, p. 1A.

29. Craig Kopp, "Dreamworks Bests on George," *Cincinnati Post*, September 25, 1997, Perspective Extra 14.

30. Ibid.

31. Craig Kopp, "Gorgeous George's Life at the Top," *Cincinnati Post*, June 25, 1998, Perspective 16.

32. Kenneth Turan, *Los Angeles Times*, September 26, 1997.

33. Sanz, "Sexiest Man Alive 1997/George Clooney."

34. Ibid.

35. Dave Larsen, "George Clooney Shoots His Mouth Off," *Dayton Daily News*, June 28, 1998, p. 1C.

36. Ibid.

37. Stephen Schaefer, "Doctor's New Orders: For ER's George Clooney, 'Out of Sight' Is a Chance at Big-Screen Redemption," *Boston Herald*, June 21, 1998, p. A&L 35.

38. Terry Lawson, "'Out of Sight' Has Clooney Fairly Crowing with Delight," *Contra Costa Times*, June 26, 1998, p. TO10.

39. Cindy Pearlman, "Dr. Feelgood: Clooney is Ready for Film Success," *Chicago Sun-Times*, June 21, 1998, Showcase 3.

40. Ibid.

41. Jamie Portman, "ER Star Dumps Little Screen for the Big One," Southam Newspapers, *The Record*, June 25, 1998, p. D9.

42. Ibid.

43. Schaefer, "Doctor's New Orders."

44. Ibid.

45. Mal Vincent, "Is Superstar Status in Sight for Clooney?" *Orlando Sentinel*, June 27, 1998, p. E9.

46. Ibid.

47. David Ansen, "The Fugitive Falls in Love: Clooney Earns His Movie-Star Stripes with 'Out of Sight,'" *Newsweek*, June 29, 1998, p. 66.

48. Craig Kopp, "Clooney Scores Big in 'Sight,'" *Cincinnati Post*, June 26, 1998, p. 1B.

49. Philip Wuntch, "Clooney Tunes Up His Career with New Film," *Dallas Morning News*, June 26, 1998, Guide, p. 7.

50. Marshall Fine, "The Screening Room/What Other Critics Are Saying," *Seattle Times*, June 26, 1998, p. G3.

51. Roger Ebert, "Comedy Before Crime: 'Out of Sight' Stops to Smell the Caper," *Chicago Sun-Times*, June 26, 1998. Weekend Plus, p. 33.

52. Elvis Mitchell, "The Director Who Got George Clooney to Act," *Fort Worth Star-Telegram*, June 26, 1998, Life & Arts 1.

53. Ibid.

54. Larsen, "George Clooney Shoots His Mouth Off."

55. Ibid.

56. Schaefer, "Doctor's New Orders."

57. Ibid.

58. Pearlman, "Dr. Feelgood."

59. Schaefer, "Doctor's New Orders."

60. *Post* news services, "George Clooney and the New Rat Pack," *Cincinnati Post*, December 7, 2001, p. 1B.

Chapter 7

GOODBYE, *ER*; HELLO, BEAUTIFUL PEOPLE

With a hit movie under his belt and the press unanimously anointing him a bona-fide movie star, not to mention his beautiful girlfriend, George Clooney found that his life was going better than he could have imagined in those days living in Aunt Rosemary's house.

All that was ahead as far as the small screen was to finish the television season of the show that had catapulted him to such success. Leaving *ER* really started with staying with *ER*. Much was written about the fact that Clooney, unlike some other high-profile TV stars who, after their fame skyrocketed, jumped from the ships that had launched them, was living up to the original five-year contract he had signed when *ER* began. But, given this man's feelings about loyalty, success, and ethics, it is hard to imagine him doing anything else.

"I'm the lowest-paid actor on the show," Clooney admitted. "The funny thing is, every time I open the paper it says, 'Oh, he gets paid $150,000 an episode.' I don't. I get paid what I got paid from the original contract. Which was fine. It's what I negotiated. I didn't go in and ask for more money. I didn't go in and ask for more time. I signed on for five years."[1]

He stayed for five years. But five years was enough.

"Five years on a drama show as the same character every single week, you've done a lot of episodes," he said, noting that the work was enjoyable partly because his costars became his friends. "We spend weekends together. It's a strange, sick relationship where people actually get along. That usually doesn't happen. I've done a lot of bad television, and there is a lot of fighting that goes on. Believe me, on *Roseanne*, we weren't all hangin' out."[2]

Though many stars pretend to like the people they work with, Clooney's words had the ring of truth, particularly because it was well known that he had gone on trips such as driving vacations with his *ER* pals.[3] Apparently, despite his breakout fame, he was still an easy guy to travel with.

"Fairly early on in my career," Clooney said, "I knew I wasn't going to be the guy who threw the fits and made life difficult and was the guy who was a jerk on the set. I honestly believe that when you turn into a jerk when you get famous, it's because fame has allowed you to be what you've been all along—and you've been keeping it quiet."[4]

Cincinnati Enquirer writer John Kiesewetter knew firsthand how much fun went on during an *ER* taping. He spent a day on the set and remembered it well.

"They were taping an episode that ran near Valentine's Day—the OB unit had a flood, so all the pregnant women were in the ER to deliver. We were watching them film and here's Doug Ross over a woman on her back with her legs up and he's reaching to birth the baby, like a quarterback calling football signals. He pulls back and launches a plastic baby across the ER," Kiesewetter said.[5]

"George said working in the studio 14 hours a day was like being in a submarine—you never get outside and look out, so they appreciated George being a cutup. He kept them loose and relieved a bit of the tension of the long, heavy duty days in the windowless environment."

Clooney sometimes put sticky surgical lubricating gel on telephones, door knobs, or even the cane used by Laura Innes's character, Dr. Weaver. He once handed Innes the cane before a scene full of technical medical dialogue.

"This goo was going through my fingers and dripping down my leg," as she spoke, she said with a laugh.[6]

The pranks helped pass the time during some long days, days that added up to five years, years during which many expected Clooney to try to escape.

"He has lost literally millions of dollars by staying on the show," *ER* executive producer John Wells told TV critics the summer before Clooney's last season on *ER*.[7]

"He probably could have—for a lot of good reasons—gotten out of his deal," said Anthony Edwards, *ER*'s Dr. Mark Greene. "He's done a very heroic thing by staying on the show."[8]

Well, "heroic" might be stretching it. But it was certainly an honorable thing to do for the show, which, cast members at the time said, would survive his departure, as it had survived the departure of other cast members previously. Besides, the show had survived Clooney's absence while he made six films in two years.

"We've had many, many episodes where he's not very prevalent," Wells said.

"In some episodes, he hasn't appeared at all, and I don't think the show has suffered," said Alex Kingston, who played Dr. Elizabeth Corday.[9] As it turned out, the show survived another nine years. In 2009, when the final season was winding down, the speculation was rampant that Clooney would return. NBC executives wouldn't confirm it, up to and including the night Dr. Ross appeared again onscreen.[10]

When Clooney's decision to leave *ER* was big news in 1999 and all his costars were being interviewed about his exit, Clooney himself declined to grant interviews, seemingly determined not to focus attention on himself and away from the show.[11]

But retrospectives of his time on the show, including stories about Clooney on the *ER* set, were all over the media. Cast and crew praised him as a regular guy, with stories such the one about the time that producers of the show tried to make the extras sit apart from the cast and crew at lunch. Clooney responded by drawing a caricature (shades of his old shoe-selling job) lampooning bossy producers and setting it up in a prominent location in the lunchroom. The rule was subsequently dropped.

"He just wanted everyone to be equal," said set decorator Michael Claypool.[12]

This was yet one more telling story about Clooney's five years as a member of a successful ensemble cast, becoming a superstar in another world, yet remaining "one of the guys." When Clooney returned to the ER set to complete shooting his final episodes, Kellie Martin was joining the ensemble drama. Clooney was the first to welcome her.

"If he was so nice, then I knew everyone was going to be nice, because he was George Clooney," she said. "He's so down-to-earth, and so much fun."[13]

On Clooney's last day of filming, his famous generosity was evident. He walked in with a box in his hand, suggesting the group have a "Dollar Day." The occasional Friday afternoon tradition was that cast and crew would throw dollar bills into a box and the person whose name was drawn got the pot—usually $100 or so. But Clooney was unusually insistent that everyone play on that day.

Crew member Steve Robertson guessed that Clooney had dropped something extra into the pot. Others guessed the same thing. "People ran to the bank to get dollar bills—I'm not kidding," Robertson said.

Sure enough, when the winner—Robertson—was announced, he took home $6,100—including a $5,000 "thanks-for-the-memories" check from Dr. Doug Ross.[14]

Nick wrote about George's final days on ER, as well.

"Our son has been proud to be a part of ER. It was never a stepping stone, always a destination, a dream role. He fulfilled his original contract to the letter. The role he created will be remembered as long as television has a place in our national memory. . . . Nina and I are proud of our son, grateful to those who gave him a chance to prove what a fine actor he is. We bid farewell to Dr. Ross with the same twinge many of you do."[15]

Nearly a year after his last episode, Clooney finally discussed his exit, saying he was not sorry he'd left the show and adding, in his self-deprecating way, "I don't have any regrets about not trying to keep reinventing the character. I was kind of running out of stuff. I'm sort of a limited actor, so it's probably best that I got out when I did. I certainly miss all of those people—it was the best time of my life and the best thing in the world for my career."[16]

ER and Clooney's career both flourished—though Clooney's career probably more so—and the press was filled with stories about his upcoming projects, both on TV and in films. Some materialized, some didn't.

Clooney had planned a semiautobiographical comedy series for HBO to be called *Kilroy*. HBO had ordered a pilot and six scripts for the comedy about a 22-year-old aspiring actor trying to make it in Hollywood. The character was supposed to visit TV studios and do bit parts on real TV shows. The idea was that Clooney would encourage his Hollywood pals to write episodes based on their own experiences. That series was scrapped a few months later.[17]

Clooney's Maysville Pictures company also planned to remake his favorite film, *Fail-Safe*, for CBS. (Maysville Pictures was named for his father's hometown, the Mason County town near Clooney's hometown of Augusta. Clooney had planned to call the company Augusta Pictures but found out that name was already being used.) The original 1964 thriller, about an accidental nuclear strike launched at the Soviet Union, starred Henry Fonda and Walter Matthau. Clooney's remake eventually became a successful reality.

Another project anticipated post-*ER* was a CBS TV-movie, *Murrow and Me*, about newsman Edward R. Murrow and Senator Joseph McCarthy in the early 1950s. That project, mentioned in various articles about Clooney for years, would eventually become a major motion picture and another turning point for Clooney.

But while America was awaiting Clooney's final appearance on the top-rated *ER*, Clooney was in Arizona completing *Three Kings*, a remake of *The Treasure of the Sierra Madre*. The update of the 1948 Humphrey Bogart classic centered on a treasure hunt during the period after the Persian Gulf war, with the Arizona desert standing in for the Middle East.

"It was grueling work for the actors and crew for months in the heat and sand of the Arizona desert," Nick Clooney wrote. "Let me hasten to add that the comments about the heat and the sand and subsequent remarks about the difficulties and discomfort of making these films are mine, not George's. He has never complained to his mother and me about location hardship. Quite the opposite. He is grateful to be working and succeeding in a profession he aspired to from childhood. It is I, as an observer, telling you how physically hard it is to do this work."[18]

Another observer, who served as a set doctor for *Three Kings* for a few days on location, agreed that the movie seemed to be hot and difficult work, but he felt that the difficulty had more to do with tension caused by the director than the weather.

"He was irritating everyone, yelling at everyone," the set doctor, John Shufeldt, said. "The film was over budget and very delayed. It was very uncomfortable being on the set."[19]

Shufeldt spent just a few days on that set, but his impressions of Clooney were strong, and exactly the opposite of his impressions of director David O. Russell. Shufeldt found Clooney sincere and down to earth. Shufeldt had dropped into a difficult situation that was whispered about at the time and, later, often written about. Russell would ask Clooney to be calm on the set, but Clooney would frequently offer his suggestions and advice. Clooney supposedly thought that Russell was mistreating the cast, and he called Warner Brothers to complain about it.[20]

Though Clooney had spent more than a decade getting along famously with nearly all of his costars on TV and in film, his difficult relationship with Russell would be something reporters asked about for years.

"David tries to sell the idea of screaming and yelling and hitting as a way to get a performance out of people," Clooney said. "But when he's screaming at a cameraman, then it's just that he's not in control."[21]

Though Clooney fought to get the part in *Three Kings*, he flatly said he would never work with Russell again.

Russell yelled "at someone daily," Clooney said. "I told him, 'You can yell and scream and even fire him, but what you can't do is humiliate him in front of people. Not on my set, if I have any say about it. It was truly, without exception, the worst experience of my life."[22]

Clooney's busy film schedule continued without one day's respite, though, if one only watched TV, one could assume he'd retired.

"Many viewers apparently thought he just drove home after his last show, closed the door, started twiddling his thumbs and waiting for something to happen," wrote Nick Clooney. "Instead, he has been immersed in some of the most interesting and difficult work of his life, with hardly a day off all year long. And there is no end in sight."[23]

In reality, George went to Mississippi and began work on Joel and Ethan Coen's *O Brother, Where Art Thou?* after wrapping *ER*. He worked in brutal heat and humidity much of the spring and summer and then finished interior scenes back in California. Next up was a tour to promote *Three Kings*; then Clooney would start work on his next picture, *The Perfect Storm*. So much for down time.

Meanwhile, another project—one close to George's heart and background—finally made it onto Clooney's schedule: the live production of *Fail-Safe* for television.

Clooney's interest in live television was not new. A few years earlier, in September 1997, *ER* had produced its first, and only, live production—mostly at Clooney's urging. Clooney's interest in live TV had been born, of course, back on Cincinnati sets when he spent all those years hanging around his father's live TV shows. Though Clooney had grown up around and understood the attraction and benefits of live television, he was working with people who had never experienced it. But the draw was there, in the back of his mind, and eventually he was in a position to get what he wanted: a live episode of *ER*. Clooney talked up his idea among his fellow actors and then went to the producers.

The unusual episode was mostly dismissed by critics as a stunt, but it attracted a lot of attention. The fourth-season premiere of *ER* went live twice: in the Eastern/Central and the Pacific time zones (in the Mountain time zone, it aired from tape). The episode went off without a major hitch, without what George Clooney had hinted he might try—a plug for his upcoming movie, *The Peacemaker*. The show got great ratings, but it probably would have whether or not it was live.

The *ER* experiment opened the door for another opportunity that Clooney had been hoping for for years—the chance to remake his favorite live TV movie. On New Year's Eve 2000, he told his parents that the live *Fail-Safe* project, something he knew his father would love, was a "go."

Nick Clooney wrote about his son's exploits in live TV in his newspaper column, with much more enthusiasm than most TV critics, noting that Cincinnati was the "last outpost of live TV" and that his son "left here as its apostle."

At the winter TV critics' press tour in Los Angeles, *Fail-Safe* was a hot topic, considering that it was to be CBS's first live drama broadcast in 40 years, since the end of *Playhouse 90* in 1960. That 90-minute dramatic TV anthology series began in 1956 and produced 133 episodes of live TV.

"Live television is great," Clooney told critics. "It's a great sort of forum to work in. We were around it my whole life. And to me, I always find it to be much more interesting . . . because of seeing how much fun my dad had."[24]

"George Clooney hopes his fond memories of his father's live Cincinnati TV shows helps revive TV's golden age of live drama," Kiesewetter wrote.[25]

Clooney told critics he hoped the black-and-white telecast would be the first of four such productions. *Fail-Safe* was a remake of the 1964 Cold War thriller about a U.S. bomber accidentally ordered to drop a nuclear warhead on Moscow. The film, Clooney said, was his all-time favorite—a movie he used to force friends to watch. He had first seen it by chance, flipping channels as a kid. "I sat there with my mouth open for the last hour of it. And I couldn't believe what I was watching," he said.[26]

The cast of *Fail-Safe* included his ex-*ER* costar Noah Wyle. Only one person offered a part in the telecast turned it down—Nick Clooney. "I said, 'Come on, come on, be a senator or something.' He won't do that. He will never do it," Clooney told TV critics.[27]

When he told his dad about his project, his dad's reaction was "Don't do it. . . . 'What are you, stoned?'—I believe was his exact phrase," Clooney said.[28] In another interview, he said, "No. He's excited. He's— it was the world that he spent—you know, from anchoring to having variety shows to pretty much everything he's done has always been circling around live television, and it's exciting to him. It's certainly where I got the bug, and it's a compliment to him because I—you know, I'm a fan of his."[29]

The reaction of the television networks to the suggestion of a live show would probably have been much like Nick Clooney's if anyone but George had asked them to provide two hours for a live production. "You needed George Clooney's power to get that kind of production on the air," CBS Television President Les Moonves said.[30]

Clooney hoped to build on the success of *ER* and *Fail-Safe* and create live productions of old TV shows, such as *The Twilight Zone*.

"If we do it right, maybe we can open up a different door for television," Clooney said.[31]

But it was not to be. In August, four months after *Fail Safe* aired to mixed but mostly positive reviews, it became clear that no future live

TV projects would be happening. Clooney had too many balls in the air, mostly because of the huge success of his blockbuster movie that summer of 2000, *The Perfect Storm*.

"After *The Perfect Storm*, I think George is going to be a $20-million-plus guy," Moonves said—obviously more money than it was possible to make in TV. Speculation also surrounded the long-talked-about TV project known as *Murrow and Me*, which Moonves had wanted Clooney to produce and star in.[32]

"Now the chances of him doing both are less and less," said Moonves, who became a friend of the actor's after Moonves, who ran Warner Brothers Television in the 1990s, hired Clooney for *Bodies of Evidence*, *Sisters*, and *ER*.[33]

Meanwhile, the chance of Clooney's being named to just about any list anyone thought up kept increasing. In June 2000, he was number one on *People*'s "100 Most Eligible Bachelors" list, not long after he'd been named to the magazine's list of "50 Most Beautiful People" in the world. "George, fresh from his live TV production of *Fail-Safe*, has earned the honor with 'the kind of nonchalant machismo that transports mature women back to the giggly thrill of prom night,'" the magazine said.[34]

Noted the *Cincinnati Post*: "The 5-foot-11 Clooney is praised for his eyelashes ('like fans') and his big brown eyes, which 'stun people when they meet him.' And he has a sense of humor, to boot."[35]

TV, movie, and magazine-list success at the highest levels—what more could he ask for?

NOTES

1. Cindy Pearlman, "Dr. Feelgood: Clooney is Ready for Film Success," *Chicago Sun-Times*, June 21, 1998, Showcase 3.

2. Ibid.

3. Stephen Schaefer, "George Clooney, 'Out of Sight' Is a Chance at Big-Screen Redemption," *Boston Herald*, June 21, 1998, p. A&L 35.

4. Ibid.

5. John Kiesewetter, phone interview with author, October 30, 2008.

6. John Kiesewetter, "Five Years on 'ER' Turned Struggling Sitcom Actor into Charismatic Star," *Cincinnati Enquirer*, February 18, 1999, p. 1C.

7. Ibid.

8. Ibid.

9. Ibid.

10. Pamela Warrick, "George Clooney Headed Back to ER," *People.com*, January 21, 2009, http://tvwatch.people.com/2009/01/21/george-clooney-headed-back-to-er/.

11. Tom Giatto, "End of an ER-a: George Clooney, That Big Operator in the Emergency Room, Hangs up His Scrubs," *People*, February 22, 1999, p. 50.

12. Ibid.

13. Kiesewetter, "Five Years on 'ER' Turned Struggling Sitcom Actor into Charismatic Star."

14. Giatto, "End of an ER-a."

15. Nick Clooney, "Dr. Ross, You're Leaving in Style," *Cincinnati Post*, February 19, 1999, p. 1B.

16. John Kiesewetter, "Clooney Won't Be Upset if He Doesn't Return to ER," *Cincinnati Enquirer*, January 16, 2000, p. F8.

17. Greg Paeth, "Goodbye, Dr. Ross: Clooney's Leaving 'ER' for New Challenges," *Cincinnati Post*, February 16, 1999, p. 1C.

18. Nick Clooney, "Life after 'ER': George Stays Busy," *Cincinnati Post*, August 27, 1999, p. 1B.

19. John Shufeldt, phone interview with author, November 17, 2008.

20. Ian Parker, "Somebody Has to Be in Control," *New Yorker*, April 14, 2008, p. 40.

21. Joel Stein, "The Wiz of Show Biz: George Clooney Knows You Think He's Slick and Pampered—And He'll Make You Like Him for It," *Time*, December 6, 2004, p. 100.

22. "Clooney Doesn't Heart Russell," excerpt of *Playboy* interview, posted at Slate.com/id/2165062.

23. Clooney, "Life after 'ER.'"

24. John Kiesewetter, "Clooney Hopes to Inject Some 'Live' into Television," *Cincinnati Post*, January 16, 2000, p. F1.

25. Ibid.

26. Ibid.

27. Greg Paeth, "Live Encore: Clooney Takes Risk with 'Fail Safe,'" *Cincinnati Post*, April 6, 2000, p. 1B.

28. Ibid.

29. Ibid.

30. John Kiesewetter, "Clooney's TV Work Victim of His Success," *Cincinnati Enquirer*, August 8, 2000, p. 4C.

31. Kiesewetter, "Clooney Hopes to Inject Some 'Live' into Television."

32. Kiesewetter, "Clooney's TV Work Victim of His Success."

33. Ibid.

34. "George Clooney: Actor/50 Most Beautiful People in the World," *People*, May 8, 2000, p. 82.

35. "Cover Boy Clooney," *Cincinnati Post*, May 4, 2000, p. 1B.

Actor George Clooney chases a loose ball during a pick-up basketball game in Gloucester, Massachusetts, Monday, September 13, 1999, during a break in the shooting of the movie The Perfect Storm. AP Photo/Lisa Poole.

Actor George Clooney listens to Tegla Loroupe, right, of Kenya respond to questions on Darfur during a news interview, Friday, December 15, 2006, at the United Nations headquarters. AP Photo/ Frank Franklin II.

Actor George Clooney puts on a crown and "Sexiest Man Alive" sash presented to him on the NBC Today television show during an interview, in New York, December 1, 2006. He tells Newsweek in its December 18, 2006, issue that he can't get any woman he wants despite being a two-time winner of People magazine's "Sexiest Man Alive." AP Photo/Richard Drew.

George Clooney, a cast member in the film Ocean's Thirteen, poses with his mother Nina at the premiere of the film at Grauman's Chinese Theatre in Los Angeles, Tuesday, June 5, 2007. AP Photo/Chris Pizzello.

Actor and new United Nations Messenger of Peace George Clooney speaks to a reporter at UN headquarters, Thursday, January 31, 2008. AP Photo/Seth Wenig.

In this February 24, 2008 picture, George Clooney arrives for the 80th Academy Awards in Los Angeles. AP Photo/Kevork Djansezian, file.

U.S.-born actress Renee Zellweger, left, and U.S. actor George Clooney pose for the presentation of their latest movie Leatherheads, in Paris, Friday, April 11, 2008. AP Photo/Francois Mori.

Chapter 8

GEORGE VERSUS
THE STALKERAZZI

As his life and career went along their successful path, it turned out there was at least one thing George Clooney didn't have a sense of humor about: paparazzi and tabloid reporters.

Things had changed a lot since the day in mid-1994 when Clooney told John Kiesewetter that he had managed to work in TV for many years without getting famous. Within weeks, he was famous. In no time, he was mega-famous, and everyone wanted a piece of him. Eventually, it took its toll, even though he was still popular with the mainstream press.

In November 1995, when Clooney attended the Cincinnati Kidney Foundation's celebration of his family, his oft-quoted previous remark about how lucky he was to be making a good living while not having to deal with celebrity was a popular topic of conversation. Now that those days were over, what was it like dealing with the microscopic attention he'd been happy to avoid?[1]

"It isn't as bad as I thought it was going to be," George said.[2]

It took about a year for Clooney to admit publicly that he'd changed his mind. "Even George Tires of Attention" was the headline in the *Cincinnati Post* in October 29, 1996. It was the paparazzi, which Clooney called the "stalkerazzi," who shadowed him wherever he went, that sparked his change of attitude.[3]

The seismic shift in Clooney's perspective would create many far-reaching tremors in the celebrity/paparazzi relationship for years. It began with Clooney's announcement, in October 1996, that he would no longer participate in interviews with TV's *Entertainment Tonight* after its sister show, *Hard Copy*, ran video of Clooney and girlfriend Celine Balitran. The video had violated a six-month-old agreement, until then unannounced, that Clooney would only appear on the interview-oriented *ET* if the tabloid *Hard Copy* left him alone. "At some point, you've got to say, 'What are you in control of?'" Clooney said. "This is kind of a warning shot."[4]

Again, the apple did not fall far from the tree. Nick Clooney—because of his sister, no stranger to the amount and intensity of press given a superstar—had written about what he called "buzzards" just 18 months earlier.

Tabloid reporters had begun coming to Augusta, Kentucky, the town where George had grown up and where Nick and Nina still lived, to interview people about George. Townspeople started out generous and willing to be interviewed, but, after a time, many felt they'd been burned, Clooney wrote. "One woman said she was so misquoted that the 'reporter' turned her meaning on its head. George became even more of a celebrity. He appeared on the cover of several major magazines. He was a guest on TV shows. He signed a deal for a movie. Buzzards began to circle Augusta again. Their mission was to rip this new TV icon to shreds. To find or, if necessary, invent some vulnerable spot."[5]

Nick Clooney, the Murrow-inspired journalist, objected to the tabloid employees calling themselves "reporters" and to their calling their publications "newspapers." As he put it, "They are not. They are a caricature of news. They attempt to destroy people and call it news. Why? And why do we watch it and read it?"[6]

It is impossible to know if George Clooney would have become a sort of point man in Hollywood's uprising against unreasonable press attention if his father had been a doctor or businessman or farmer instead of a hard-nosed traditional journalist. But Nick's attitude toward the tabloid press and its questionable rights obviously rubbed off on his son and perhaps emboldened even big Hollywood names to stand up and rebel.

Within days of George Clooney's announced boycott of *Hard Copy*, other stars backed him up—heavy hitters like Whoopi Goldberg, Madonna, and Steven Spielberg, for starters. Like everything else Clooney, George's boycott of tabloids got a lot of press, including from his dad, who noted that his son's boycott seemed a small story to be getting so much attention.

"But the matter may have important consequences for the profession of journalism—*Hard Copy* is one of an insidious wave of such programs that has afflicted the public; infected the business of news; and, in my opinion, lowered the bar of truth and civility in our society for a decade," Nick wrote.[7]

Celebrities certainly give up some claim to privacy, Nick Clooney acknowledged, but he felt strongly that the media shouldn't assume they have no right to decency and fair treatment. His son agreed.

"Look, I'm the luckiest guy in the world. But if people tell lies about me, insult the young woman I am with, using the coarsest language you can imagine in an attempt to get me mad enough so they can have a tape they can sell to *Hard Copy*, it seems to me I have a right to respond," George said.[8]

The out-of-control situation celebrities were dealing with at that time became a big news story. "The actor objected to the invasion of his private life by so-called stalkerazzi—a new breed of relentlessly intrusive, often abusive, still and video photographers who make their living by cursing out, spying on, shoving or even spitting at celebrities and then selling the resulting images to tabloid TV and magazines."[9]

Six months earlier—though it was not reported at that time—George Clooney had sent a letter to Paramount Television Group, which produced *Entertainment Tonight* and *Hard Copy*, to complain about the increasingly untenable situation. The result was an agreement in writing between Frank H. Kelly, president of creative affairs for Paramount Pictures, and Clooney, which he kept quiet at that time. "We agree that *Hard Copy* will not be covering you. I am also going to look into the practices you referred to regarding video 'paparazzi'—these people may still try to sell footage to other programs, but at least they will not have our shows as outlets," Kelly pledged.[10]

So, when, in October, *Hard Copy*, despite its promise, used a video-tape obtained from paparazzi, George wrote to Paramount Television to say he would no longer appear on *Entertainment Tonight*.

"George Clooney, tired of being haunted by paparazzi's videocams, tried playground tactics: when a bully picks on you, stop dating his sister," *Time* wrote. When the deal between Kelly and Clooney was broken by *Hard Copy*, Clooney discussed the until-then private agreement in public and noted his own "gotcha" moment.

"A so-called news format show will agree that they will not be covering me in any future stories, if I do his other show," his letter to *ET* said. "Now that's amazing."[11]

Clooney's comments echoed his father's column, in which Nick expressed disbelief that any show professing to be a news show would make such an agreement with a potential news subject. "Imagine the president of ABC, CBS, NBC, CNN or any other genuine news organization making a similar deal. It would mean their jobs and might fatally damage their news operations," Clooney wrote.[12]

Proof, both Clooneys claimed, that *Hard Copy* is not a news show and has no legitimate journalistic rights. George made a point of supporting the freedom of even a show like *Hard Copy* to be whatever kind of show it wants. But he drew the line at accepting that he had to cooperate with tabloid operations the way he did with respected journalistic outlets.[13]

"I understand I'm a celebrity," George Clooney said. "I make a good living, I don't ask anybody to feel sorry for me and I don't expect anyone to. But I think that we all should be afforded certain civil rights, and some of them are you can't put bounties on people's head and have people try to jump in your window for $300,000 to get a picture of you and your baby," he said, referring to an episode that occurred after the pop singer Madonna gave birth.[14]

It wasn't long before Paramount agreed to stop airing footage on *Hard Copy* that had been obtained through insults and harassment used "solely to provide a reaction." It also promised not to use "unauthorized footage" of stars at home or "footage that is known to have been obtained illegally."

"Although celebrities have chosen a profession that puts them in the public eye, we feel that coverage of their lives should not extend to other than public venues," Paramount Pictures Television Group said.[15]

Once Paramount made that announcement, Clooney said he would videotape the TV tabloids nightly to police them. "My responsibility now," Clooney said, "and the hard part of this, is to monitor it and stay on top of it and see if there are any changes at all. I don't want to belittle what has happened, what Paramount was willing to do. I think it's great. But if it were just left up to its own devices, I don't know that anything would change and there would be any difference at all."[16]

The discussion of paparazzi behavior was to explode again worldwide in the near future. But first, the ABC-TV News show *Turning Point* did a program in which it examined paparazzi through history. In preparing the show, Robert Krulwich interviewed Nick Clooney. Krulwich repeated the paparazzis' belief that celebrities choose to be in the public eye and that their being stalked in public is a natural and reasonable outcome of that choice.

"Says who?" wrote Clooney later in a column. "Because this tasteless moral bankrupt proclaims it does that make it true? I don't think so. Certainly, every person who finds himself or herself in a public profession understands there will be increased recognition and scrutiny. There will be public events at which he or she will be expected to respond to those who support them. But are they never to have a private dinner again? Never go to the movies with their kids or take them to school, shop with their spouses, bring their newborn home from the hospital without these crude intrusions?"[17]

Through history, Nick Clooney noted, society itself had become more interested in seeing the results of such tabloid "journalism." He wrote, "Why did news used to more civil? Because all the rest of us were more civil, that's why."[18]

Perhaps. But that summer, a tragedy intensified the conversation. Britain's Princess Diana and two others were killed in an automobile accident while being chased by paparazzi. George Clooney's anti-paparazzi profile was raised even higher.

"My son, actor George Clooney, has been in a very public dispute with tabloid and paparazzi for more than a year. When watching coverage [of Diana's death] over the weekend, I recalled an interview with him on the subject. The reporter asked, 'When will this frenzy end?'

George answered, 'When somebody dies.' Somebody has died. Will the frenzy end? Is this, finally, enough?" Nick wrote in his column.[19]

George Clooney tried to explain the difference between stalkers who follow celebrities' every move and who attempt to create news and censorship of the paparazzi, which he vehemently condemned. The type of thing Clooney objected to was situations like this one: "You're harassed," he said. "I have a daily problem with people harassing me—harassing me!—trying to get you into a fight, following you to restaurants, following you to dinner."[20]

The difference, as Clooney saw it, was to differentiate between the mainstream press and tabloid stalking.[21] After Diana died, suddenly "I'm the spokesman against tabloid television; suddenly I'd become the spokesperson against paparazzi. And if you read any quote I'd said, I kept saying that the only thing worse than an irresponsible bunch of schmucks with cameras is trying to censor those irresponsible schmucks," Clooney said.[22] He added, "The unfortunate deal about the idea of freedom of press is that they aren't necessarily going to be fair a lot of the time. But you have to take that. So I was suddenly the spokesperson. And I got called, and everybody was asking if I wanted to talk about this. And I was, like, 'No, this has nothing to do with what I've been fighting.'"[23]

But did Clooney wish he could avoid more of the publicity of his job?

"Yeah, oh, sure. It's a weird tradeoff. The fun part about acting or directing is the actual doing of it, and then almost everything else about it strangely isn't fun. You don't really get it until you're inside that inner circle, that all the things you thought would be great when you're famous—a premiere or some sort of notoriety—that's not really fun. I don't want to say it's awful; it's not awful—. . . .You're at a bar, and there's 50 people trying to get to you, to talk to you, and some guy's going, 'This must be great, dude!' And you're, like, 'This is so not great.'"

Clooney added, "But what is great is the idea that you can walk into a studio in 2003 and say, 'We're going to make a film about oil corruption, and we're going to talk about what makes a suicide bomber.' And to be able to walk into a studio and say this is what we're going to do and have them say, 'Okay,' well, that's why you do this. That's a good time."[24]

A year after Diana's death, not much had changed.

"There isn't a day that goes by that absolute, complete lies and fabrications are [sic] printed about me. I'll read, the other day, I was in the Bahamas at Cindy Crawford's wedding and I'm sitting with Richard Gere. I'm in New York reading this. And I've got good friends of mine calling and saying, 'Hey, how was the Bahamas?' Now, that doesn't hurt anybody. It's innocuous, but there are ones that aren't."[25]

Years later, Clooney the lifelong prankster thought of a way to have fun and strike back at the paparazzi, who often found out where to go to photograph celebrities through Web sites such as Gawker.com's "Gawker Stalker" feature. In April 2006, Clooney's publicist, Stan Rosenfield, distributed a letter from Clooney to other stars' publicists suggesting a way their clients could fight back against the site which some felt was a threat to them.

"There is a simple way to render these guys useless," Clooney's message said. "Fool their Web site with bogus sightings. Get your clients to get 10 friends to text in fake sightings of any number of stars. A couple hundred conflicting sightings and this Web site is worthless. No need to try to create new laws to restrict free speech. Just make them useless. That's the fun of it. And then sit back and enjoy the ride." The letter was signed, "Thanks, George."

Over the years, George Clooney has spoken often about fame and has seemed quite comfortable with his fame. But, as his struggles with stalkers makes obvious, sometimes even he has felt the need to protect his privacy. In Italy, he went so far as to buy the house next to his own property to keep the paparazzi away.[26]

NOTES

1. Mary Jo DiLonardo, "Reflections on an Evening with a Certain Clooney," *Cincinnati Post*, November 15, 1995, p. 1C.

2. Ibid.

3. "Even George Tires of Attention," *Cincinnati Post*, October 29, 1996, p. 12A.

4. Ibid.

5. Nick Clooney, "George's Fame Draws Buzzards," *Cincinnati Post*, May 1, 1995, p. 1B.

6. Ibid.

7. Nick Clooney, "George versus the Tabloid Dragons," *Cincinnati Post*, November 1, 1996, p. 1B.

8. Ibid.

9. Peter Castro, "Stalking Heads: Fed up and Fighting Back, Celebs Face Down the Paparazzi Who Hound Them," *People*, November 25, 1996, p. 71.

10. Clooney, "George versus the Tabloid Dragons."

11. "George Clooney Decides to Play Hardball," *Time*, November 11, 1996, p. 101.

12. Clooney, "George versus the Tabloid Dragons."

13. Ibid.

14. Associated Press, "In War on Trash TV, Clooney Is General: 'Hard Copy' Battle Just the Beginning," *Cincinnati Post*, November 13, 1996, p. 1A.

15. Ibid.

16. Ibid.

17. Nick Clooney, "Only We Can Stop Prying Cameras," *Cincinnati Post*, January 15, 1997, p. 1C.

18. Ibid.

19. Nick Clooney, "Will Diana's Death End the Madness?" *Cincinnati Post*, September 3, 1997, p. 1C.

20. Craig Kopp, "Dreamworks Bets on George," *Cincinnati Post*, September 25, 1997, Perspective Extra 14.

21. Dotson Rader, "It's Finally about Friendship and Loyalty," *Parade*, June 7, 1998, p. 4.

22. Jenelle Riley, "A Chat with One of Hollywood's Biggest Names," *Cincinnati Post*, January 3, 2006, p. B1.

23. Ibid.

24. Ibid.

25. Craig Kopp, "Gorgeous George's Life at the Top," *Cincinnati Post*, June 25, 1998, Perspective 16.

26. Ian Parker, "Somebody Has to Be in Control," *New Yorker*, April 14, 2008. p. 40.

Chapter 9

HISTORY STUDENT

They say those who ignore history are doomed to repeat it. George Clooney considered his history and learned from it, therefore repeating his successes.

During the years Clooney had jobs on TV but wanted to be a film actor, he always called himself a film actor. But, after losing a big part in a film, he decided he was a television actor, so he ought to do better television.[1] That was the decision that led him to fight for a part in *ER* rather than take another cop show being developed for him. Doing better television, of course, opened doors for Clooney to do more movies. But not necessarily better movies.

"Then I started doing sort of the same mistakes in film, which is I'd just take a job, a job and a job," just to keep working. That path led to movies such as *Batman & Robin*. Remembering his past in TV, he then decided he would "do better films," Clooney said. "It's mostly about working with better people, working with better scripts. That's usually the difference."[2]

Clooney spent the early years of the new millennium proving that point. In fairly rapid succession, three Clooney movies premiered to solid reviews: *Three Kings*, in October 1999; *The Perfect Storm*, in June

2000; and O *Brother, Where Art Thou?* in December 2000. (He also had an unbilled cameo in the 2001 *Spy Kids*, helping out the movie's writer-director, Robert Rodriguez, a friend.)[3]

In the year before he turned 40, Clooney had clearly found his groove. Critics agreed that he broke out with the satiric Gulf War adventure *Three Kings* and established box-office draw with *The Perfect Storm*. *O Brother*, the Coen brothers' take on Homer's *Odyssey*, was a departure for Clooney, giving him the chance to shine as a "modern rapscallion who would have been at home in the screwball comedies of Preston Sturges."[4] Meanwhile, the personality that had been endearing him to people since he was a kid was helping him to create warm camaraderie on his movie sets. According to *People*, "Clooney has charmed fans and crew on the Atlantic seaboard (for *Storm*,) in the Arizona desert (for *Three Kings*) and in Jackson, Miss. (*O Brother*)."[5]

The busy time illustrated two points about Clooney's life—that he enjoyed each movie set every day, winning friends and fans wherever he went (playing basketball with the crew during filming breaks on *O Brother* and hanging out with patrons at a local tavern in Gloucester, Massachusetts) and that the busy pace of his life at that point was part of the reason he and Balitran broke up.

"I kept sort of taking jobs and the jobs kept taking me further and further away," Clooney said.[6]

The role of Special Forces Captain Archie Gates in the black comedy/adventure *Three Kings*, set during the Gulf War of 1991, was one Clooney had to fight for, not unlike his efforts to become Doug Ross on *ER*. Writer/director David O. Russell needed to be convinced to lower the age of the character so that Clooney could play the role. Clooney at first believed he wouldn't get the part, but he was drawn to the script and kept fighting.[7]

Besides the great script, Clooney wanted to play a flawed, more complicated character than he had played so far. "My character starts out to do something wrong and ends up doing the right thing," he said. "That's great old story-telling: to be conned into doing the right thing."[8]

The Perfect Storm, which critic Roger Ebert called "a well-crafted example of a film of pure sensation," was Clooney's first real popular success. It was also Clooney's first time portraying someone who was real—the captain of fishing boat the Andrea Gail—and the task concerned him. "There's just a far greater sense of responsibility," Clooney said. "This isn't just a popcorn film. You do have a responsibility not to take advantage. It's that simple."[9]

The film's premiere was held in the summer of 2000 in Gloucester, Massachusetts, the home port of the crew on the ship. It would be the first time Clooney had seen the family of the ship's crew since filming the previous fall, and he was noticeably worried about how they'd react to the film, hoping they'd feel that he'd honored Captain Billy Tyne in his performance.[10]

Afterward, Tyne's sister Roberta told Clooney's mother she liked the way George had portrayed her brother.[11]

"She was on the brink of tears and when I took her hand I could feel her shaking. After nine years the loss was still fresh. Later, she and George talked to Billy's two children. The movie had brought that 1991 day back as if it were yesterday. The consensus? Roberta said, 'They stayed true to the story. This was not a movie we didn't recognize.' On the way back George was quiet for a moment. Then he told me how hard it was to see Billy's children crying. I knew what he meant."[12]

Six months later, another premiere—this one for *O Brother, Where Art Thou?*, for which Clooney would be nominated for a Golden Globe award. Clooney wanted a part in the Depression-era road-trip comedy without knowing much about the character he would play; he just wanted to work with the men who were making the film: Ethan and Joel Coen.

"The idea of getting a chance to work with guys like this was a thrill," Clooney said. "They sent the script and before I read it, I said yes. When I did read it, I thought it was a hysterically funny and smart script, I couldn't believe how lucky I was."[13]

Then he took his luck to Las Vegas, for a movie that was to be his biggest commercial success yet—the remake of the Rat Pack movie *Ocean's Eleven*, which had starred Frank Sinatra, Dean Martin, and Sammy Davis Jr.

Clooney's character, Danny Ocean, masterminds an ambitious casino heist. Frank Sinatra played the part in the original film, leaving what many assumed were big shoes for Clooney to fill. Clooney believed otherwise.

"In pre-production, people are coming up and saying, 'So you're playing Frank Sinatra.' And I'd go, 'No, I'm not playing Frank Sinatra.

I'm doing a movie that he did," Clooney said. "The truth is we had a really good script. Frank didn't get to say the lines I get to say in this movie, and he didn't get the director I got. So I won't be as cool as Frank, but I will have a better piece of material to work with. So I figured I'd be all right."[14]

The project was the first for Clooney's and Steven Soderbergh's new production company, Section Eight. The two Hollywood powerhouses had had similar missteps in the mid-1990s—Clooney with *Batman & Robin*, Soderbergh with *The Underneath*. But 1998's *Out of Sight* was a turning point for both of them, and that film clearly had made a Clooney fan out of Soderbergh.

"He's just sort of unique right now. There's no one quite like him, his age, who can do the kinds of things he does. That's probably why he gets offered everything," Soderbergh said. "And as he himself says, 'What I'm concerned about now is the films I leave behind.' He's in the fortunate position not to really have to worry about money, so he can focus on that."[15]

But even those with money have problems to focus on, particularly when some would take advantage of their money. In October 2002, Clooney had to fire his agent, Michael Gruber, for allegedly using his longtime relationship with Clooney "to cut a deal for himself. Gruber was forced to resign from the powerhouse Creative Artists Agency after Clooney learned that his agent had tried to obtain a 'finder's fee' of as much as $250,000 from the sellers of an Italian lakeside villa the actor was buying," according to a story in the *Cincinnati Post*.[16]

Negotiations for the 25-room, 18th-century, $10 million "Villa Oleandra"[17] took longer than Clooney expected, and when Clooney asked why, he was told about Gruber's request. Clooney felt that discussion of any such fee was inappropriate. That same attitude carried over into his life at the villa on Lake Como, where his neighbors learned to respect the American movie star and talk about him much the same way his friends from Augusta, Kentucky, did. Stories of his shooting baskets with the local kids, helping older ladies with their groceries, and acting like an all-around "bravo," or good person, abound.

"He's good and kind with everyone," Giordano Saibene said. "Maybe because none of us ever bothered him, he would invite us" to join him on the basketball court.[18]

During the summers, Clooney threw nightly dinners at the six-house compound, featuring such guests as former vice president Al Gore, legendary news anchor Walter Cronkite, and director Quincy Jones.

"He's an excellent host," director Tony Gilroy said. "He's really smart about figuring out what people need and want."[19]

He even brought his grandmother, Dica Warren, 85, simply because she'd never been to Europe.[20] The Italian villa became Clooney's one respite from what had become his larger-than-life life, a life that consisted of movie after movie after movie. The list included the next two produced by Section Eight—the low-key *Welcome to Collinwood*, in which he appeared only briefly and then *Solaris*, a critically acclaimed psychological science-fiction film that audiences turned their backs on.

"My feeling is seven, eight years from now, there will be people who rediscover that film, and that's OK," Clooney said. "People didn't get *Out of Sight* at all, in fact it lost money, and now people talk about it as a really good film. *O Brother* they didn't get and *Three Kings* they didn't get. And I find those films hold up. My feeling is, it's sort of better to just do them and let them sit there and pick up the pieces all at the end."[21]

The biggest news about *Solaris* was its original R rating, caused by a somewhat lengthy lingering shot of Clooney's naked backside in a love scene with Natascha McElhone. The rating was eventually downgraded to PG-13.

The unusual movie—Clooney plays a psychologist at some time in the future who is sent to treat workers on a space station and finds they are mad—wasn't aiming for huge audiences, Clooney said, but Section Eight was trying to reach for a higher plane with studio filmmaking.[22] Though the film earned a disappointing $6.8 million in its first weekend, coming in seventh, it was considered a self-indulgent film in the mode of movies from Clooney's favorite era, 1965–1975.

Soderbergh, who said Clooney is a better actor than he believes he is,[23] felt that Clooney's role in *Solaris* was comparable to Jack Nicholson's breakthrough success in *Five Easy Pieces*. "In my mind, this puts him in a totally different category," Soderbergh said.[24]

Clooney used the pain of losing his aunt Rosemary (who died in 2002) to deepen the character. Roles such as that one, he said, were important for the survival of his career in the long run. "Movie-star status lasts about 30 seconds," said Clooney, who had seen exactly that happen to his aunt. His goal, he often said, was to build a career with staying power, like Paul Newman's. Of course, if the acting gig were to run out of steam, there was always the chance he could actually use that old director's chair he had in his Cincinnati apartment.[25]

Preemptively and, at first, tentatively, he did use it, starting with *Confessions of a Dangerous Mind*, a bizarre look at the life of the late Chuck Barris, host of the *Gong Show* and a CIA hit man, which opened at the end of 2002. The job came to him almost by accident.

"I loved the screenplay and thought it wasn't going to get made," he said. "There was a feeling that if I came on board and directed it for [bottom-scale wages] and got some A-list actors to work for virtually nothing, then we thought they'd make the movie."[26] The $29 million film also starred Julia Roberts and Drew Barrymore and intrigued the majority of the critics, if not the moviegoing public.

"A blast from beginning to end and shows first-time director George Clooney is equal parts fearless, brilliant and perhaps daft. But an intriguing daftness it is," wrote Tom Long of the *Detroit News*, in what could be a description of Clooney's personality, as well.[27] According to *People*, Clooney "delivered an edgy, nuanced, remarkably assured drama."[28]

Days after the film opened, Clooney told the press he'd had fun but wouldn't be directing again in the near future. "I have to go make a living somewhere," he said as the film was screened at the Palm Springs International Film Festival. Being in the film made it more complicated. "It was a little harder than I thought it would be. You can't yell at the director when you're acting," he said.[29]

But within a couple of weeks, he was backing off that statement, saying he might direct again if another story came up that he had a unique capacity to understand. Game-show creator and host Chuck Barris was part of an environment that was familiar to Clooney from his years watching productions of the *Nick Clooney Show* leave the set where *Bowling for Dollars* would enter next.

"I knew what those sets looked like from the back and I knew how they felt, what they looked like when cameras weren't on. I certainly understand the trappings of celebrity," Clooney said. "So I thought I had a unique take on this. And if I have another film like that, I'd do it. But only if there's a reason to."[30]

Sitting down in the director's chair for the first time, Clooney admitted he borrowed techniques from the best to figure out what to do after that. From the Coen brothers, who directed Clooney in *O Brother, Where Art Thou?*, he adopted the tactic of using the "camera as a character." He took cues on "nonlinear storytelling" from Steven Soderbergh. But more important influences—"the guys I was ripping off, to be quite honest"—were Mike Nichols and Alan Pakula.[31] At least he actually had the good manners to send handwritten apology notes to those directors whose scenes he borrowed.

Another secret to his success, he hinted, was working with the same professionals over and over, as repertory companies do. He named Don Cheadle and Mark Wahlberg as repeat stars and noted he'd like to add Renee Zellweger to that list. "I'm a firm believer in working with people you like and trust," he said, exposing that pull toward the loyalty he treasured in friends, as well. For future scripts, however, he said he and Soderbergh would use a simple yardstick, and simply look for well-written screenplays.[32]

After *Confessions* and the Coen Brothers' *Intolerable Cruelty*, Clooney and his gang from *Ocean's Eleven* made the sequel, *Ocean's 12*, which opened late in 2004. Entertainment magazines noted that his escorts to that premiere included his mother and his girlfriend, Lisa Snowden, a British actress Clooney had been dating since September 2000.

But Clooney's visit to the premiere of *Ocean's 12* was not completely what it seemed. He was in pain from an injury he had suffered weeks earlier while filming *Syriana*, the extent of which was kept quiet for a while.

Clooney's publicist, Stan Rosenfield, told the press at the time he was suffering from a ruptured disk, which kept him from promoting *Ocean's 12*. Clooney had to cancel appearances in late November 2004 on *Good Morning, America*, *The Daily Show*, and *Charlie Rose*. Rosenfield told reporters Clooney's condition had worsened and that he was unable to travel, but he declined to provide details.[33]

That injury marked the beginning of a very tough year, from approximately October 2004 through October 2005, for George Clooney. It was during this time that his grandmother and his brother-in-law died, his father lost his congressional race, and his dog was killed by a rattlesnake, despite Clooney's beating off the snake with a baseball bat. He had no commercially successful movies and during *Syriana*'s filming suffered what actually was a debilitating spinal injury, which caused massive headaches. It had been, simply, the worst year of his life.[34]

One minor bright spot, sure to at least make his fans smile: *Vanity Fair* put Clooney on its best-dressed list, commenting on his "signature look—no tie, collar open, beautiful suit." (Apparently that "no tie, collar open" look he started in his eighth-grade graduation photo worked for him and stuck.)

But that year was filled with other disappointments, as well: he and Snowden broke up in June, and his HBO series, *Unscripted*—a half-hour improvised series that grew out of the *Kilroy* concept—began and was canceled, its first episode airing in January and the final episode airing on February 27. Clooney had also directed the series about three struggling actors, which was produced by Section Eight, enduring the humiliating Hollywood audition process. "It was a fun, experimental show that ran its course," an HBO spokesman said. *Newsweek* was more blunt: "The problem with *Unscripted* is a simple one: it's boring."[35]

During that down year, Clooney found out the truth of the cliché "When you have your health, you have everything." His *Syriana* injury came while he was filming a scene in which his CIA character was being tortured, but for months the public didn't know the extent of his injuries. It wasn't until a year after it occurred that Clooney's family began talking about how serious it was; Clooney had endured a tear to the dura mater, the membrane that holds spinal fluid that surrounds the brain and the spinal cord.

Clooney didn't realize he'd been hurt at the time. Migraine headaches began days later and doctors didn't pinpoint the cause of the pain at first.

"It was scary," Nick Clooney said. "When he called and said, 'stuff's coming out of my nose, pop, and I don't know what it is.'"[36] In fact, spinal fluid was being released into Clooney's brain cavity, and excess fluid was coming out through his nose. Originally, it was thought his injury had occurred when he fell back on the floor while tied to a chair. Later, however, another part of the scene was suspected—when Clooney's head was snapped one way and then the other, over and over, over two days during the filming of the torture scene.

Clooney's parents went to care for their son in California at the time because the leaking fluid caused headaches so debilitating, he couldn't get out of bed.[37] "It was kept quiet and I'm glad it was," Nick Clooney said. "His friends brought chicken soup and sat with him for long periods of time."[38]

It took major surgery and injections of blood into the dura to repair the tears. George slowly improved, but the headaches remained to plague Clooney through the filming of his next project, *Good Night and Good Luck.*

Though it was reported at that time that George had recovered, in later years he referred to the injury occasionally, noting that his health was never the same afterward and that pain had lingered in various ways for many years. He continued to have problems with his back and with short-term memory loss as late as 2008.[39]

NOTES

1. "Clooney's Making 'Same Mistakes,'" *Cincinnati Post*, December 12, 2001, p. 16C.

2. Ibid.

3. Tom Cunneff, "Insider," *People*, April 30, 2001, p. 47.

4. Post news services, "George Clooney and the New Rat Pack," *Cincinnati Post*, December 7, 2001, p. 1B.

5. Susan Schindehette, "Too Busy for Love? The Word on George Clooney's Busted Romance? Friends Say He Just Didn't Have Time," *People*, September 27, 1999, p. 119.

6. Ibid.

7. Joshua Mooney, "George Clooney Goes for the Gold," *Cincinnati Post*, September 30, 1999, Perspective Extra 5.

8. Ibid.

9. Craig Kopp, "George Clooney's Wet Look," *Cincinnati Post*, June 29, 2000, p. TO3.

10. Nina Clooney, "Premiere's 2 Scenes Contrast," *Cincinnati Post*, July 7, 2000, p. 1C.

11. Ibid.

12. Ibid.

13. "O Brother: Clooney Meets the Coens," *Cincinnati Post*, January 11, 2001, p. TO3.

14. "George Clooney and the New Rat Pack."

15. Ibid.

16. "Clooney Fires Agent," *Cincinnati Post*, October 23, 2002, p. C14.

17. "Giorgio at Play," *People*, June 16, 2003, p. 78.

18. Frances DiEmilio, "Movie Star Clooney Strives to Be 'Bravo,'" *Cincinnati Post*, July 13, 2004, p. A1.

19. Joel Stein, "Guess Who Came to Dinner?" *Time*, March 3, 2008, p. 46.

20. "Giorgio at Play."

21. Margaret A. McGurk. "In 'Confessions,' Clooney 'Stole' the Best Scenes," *Cincinnati Enquirer*, January 19, 2003, p. E1.

22. Ron Dicker, "Clooney Won't Complain about 'Solaris,'"—He Has Too Much Good Going for Him," *Cincinnati Post*, December 5, 2002, p. T5.

23. "Renaissance Man," *People*, December 30, 2002, p. 70.

24. Dicker, "Clooney Won't Complain about 'Solaris.'"

25. Ibid.

26. "In the Director's Chair," *Cincinnati Post*, December 30, 2002, p. C12.

27. Tom Long, "Clooney Makes Audacious Directing Debut with Yarn about Chuck Barris' Life," *Detroit News*, January 24, 2003, p. IE.

28. "Renaissance Man."

29. "Actor Clooney to Stick to Day Job," *Cincinnati Post*, January 6, 2003, p. C10.

30. McGurk, "In 'Confessions,' Clooney 'Stole' the Best Scenes."

31. Ibid.

32. Ibid.

33. "Clooney Sidelined," *Cincinnati Post*, November 30, 2004, p. C14.

34. Los Angeles Times, "For George, '05 Could Have Been Better," *Cincinnati Post*, October 3, 2005, p. B2.

35. Devin Gordon, "Hollywood Unplugged—Clooney's Improvised Drama about Struggling Actors," *Newsweek*, January 10, 2005, p. 55.

36. Rick Bird. "George's Injury on the Set Was Debilitating," *Cincinnati Post*, December 8, 2005, p. T15.

37. Ibid.

38. Ibid.

39. Stein, "Guess Who Came to Dinner?"

Chapter 10

GOOD LUCK

The awful year that began in October 2004 ended resoundingly in late 2005 with the opening of two movies that again would change Clooney's career.

The first was the one to which Clooney had been connected for years, one that again was a topic important to his father, one that popped up in countless newspaper stories about TV projects he was considering—a movie often referred to as *Murrow and Me*, about one event in the life of legendary news anchor Edward R. Murrow.

Somewhere along the way it became *Good Night, and Good Luck,* a black-and-white film that tells the story of Murrow's CBS broadcasts in 1953–1954 that targeted Senator Joseph McCarthy of Wisconsin and his battle against those he considered communists. The period piece takes place mostly in a smoke-filled newsroom and in studios where Murrow and his team move ahead with a story they believe in but that they know poses a danger for their careers.

Of course, that same general description could be used for some things that had already happened in Clooney's career.

George Clooney, onetime failed TV-pilot king, onetime Batman, produced, directed, cowrote (with friend and producer Grant Heslov) and costarred in the movie, which was made only because of his determination and courage in putting up his own money to tell the story the way he wanted it to be told. The most important thing to Clooney about this project was, as his father cautioned him, getting his facts straight.

The project was so close to George Clooney's heart that when he couldn't get Hollywood executives as interested in the project as he was, he put up part of the $7.5 million cost and cowrote the script. "In order to win nonmarquee actor David Strathairn the starring role in *Good Night*, Clooney agreed to play the supporting part of CBS News chief Fred Friendly," according to the *Hollywood Reporter*.[1]

"I cast myself to pay for the film. That's part of the deal," said Clooney, who paid himself $1 for the acting role. "I'm at the point now where I don't have to make money. After a certain amount of money, you don't need more. So then it comes down to what is your legacy going to be? What are you going to stand for when you get hit by a bus? You want to be able to say you made a couple of good movies."[2]

The film's completion bond (an insurance policy that a film will be finished) company yanked its policy because it feared that Clooney's back problems earlier in the year would keep him from finishing it. To get the policy reinstated, Clooney put up his home, valued at $7 million.[3] He figured it really wasn't a risk.

"The only thing that could go wrong is I couldn't finish the film. And there's no way, no way, that was going to happen unless I died," he said with a laugh. "And if I did die, hey, I wouldn't really need the house anyway."[4]

As with so many things in Clooney's life and career, the project had a strong link to his father and to his childhood. Murrow was his father's hero, a role model so ubiquitous that his photo sits on Nick and Nina's mantel at their home. Murrow was "someone my father always talked about and quoted," George said. "That showdown [with McCarthy, the subject of the movie] was very famous in our family. As proud of Murrow as my father was is how proud I am of my father, so I felt like [the movie] was in many ways a tip of the hat to the old man."[5]

"He had guts," Nick said of Murrow. "We talked about Murrow all the time and that the only thing that really matters is courage. Nina and I knew that wherever we were, the schools probably weren't going to deal with this very much."[6]

As a kid, Nick used to listen to Murrow's newscasts on the radio during World War II, and he long considered him the ultimate newsman. But even newsmen on a pedestal need to take some time out for bill-paying fluff, as the movie made clear. Murrow's position as host of *Person to Person*, a TV show on which he interviewed celebrities in order to rack up "points" to keep his hard-hitting news show, *See It Now*, on the air, figures prominently in the plot.

The parallels between Murrow's reality and George Clooney's career were frequently drawn when the movie premiered—Clooney's willingness to star in big-money crowd pleasers such as *Batman & Robin* and *Ocean's Eleven* gave him the clout and the bankroll to make the movies and TV shows he believed in, including *Good Night, and Good Luck* (Murrow's famous sign-off line).

The movie opened to rave reviews at the New York and Venice film festivals; reviews were excellent, and—most rewardingly to both Clooneys—even hard-nosed journalists liked the film. Years earlier, while Nick was working at American Movie Classics, he polled a group of high-profile journalists and asked them to rate movies about the news business. They cited just three movies, *The Front Page*, *All the President's Men*, and *Broadcast News*, as good examples of the genre, though even those films all received some mixed reviews from those polled. But when *Good Night, and Good Luck* was screened for some of the most famous journalists in news history, those in attendance gave it resounding approval ratings.

Andy Rooney said, "Gee, Nick, I thought it would be lousy. It was a good movie." Well, that's what passes for enthusiasm from a curmudgeon-y newsperson.[7] What did George's father, that guy who used to work at American Movie Classics, think?

"George got closer to what the news racket is all about than any [movie] I've ever seen," Nick wrote. "It is as close as you can get to a newsroom hot on the trail of a story. . . . You bet I really am proud."[8]

Nonrelated movie reviewers were even more effusive: "Do you respect the corporate line or do you cross it? Clooney, who in his life wears the hats both of the entertainer and the 'actorvist,' gives us an intelligent, electric film that knows this question is as timely now as it was for Murrow," wrote Carrie Rickey of the *Philadelphia Inquirer*.[9]

And how. There was no mistaking how the decades-old themes reso-nated in 2005, the post-9/11 era of "homeland security." The movie drew "a parallel between communists and terrorists, loyalty oaths and the Patriot Act and the Iraqi war critics who have had their patriotism questioned as those who questioned McCarthy were impugned," com-mented Rick Bird in the *Cincinnati Post*.[10] David Denby, in his review of the film in *The New Yorker*, said that Clooney managed to critique the world of corporate-controlled media and its apparent loyalty to the Bush administration.[11]

There was also no mistaking something else other reviewers noted: with *Good Night, and Good Luck*, Clooney's career advanced to yet an-other level. Amy Biancolli of the *Houston Chronicle* said the film put Clooney up there with "history's great directors."[12] Rex Reed of the *New York Observer* called the film "mesmerizing" and Clooney's direc-tion self-assured.[13] And Richard Roeper of *Ebert & Roper* commented, "I found it to be one of most intelligent and insightful movies ever made about the television news business and about the profoundly un-American practice of labeling dissenters as traitors."[14]

Clooney clearly found the universally glowing reactions to the film satisfying. "The fights to keep entertainment from pushing news off the air still exist," he said. "The questions about the government using fear to attack civil liberties still exist—the Patriot Act and Guantanamo Bay certainly are examples of that . . . Keeping [the movie] in a histori-cal reference like that—and being very careful with our facts, which we were—was important, so it cannot be a political, polarizing piece. It's simply a piece to raise debate and constantly talk about issues. Which I think is a good thing."[15]

Frequent comments about Clooney's tendency to choose projects with limited commercial potential sparked one of Clooney's typical keep-me-off-the-pedestal replies, which somehow is reminiscent of his comment regarding his Aunt Rosemary's posh mansion in Beverly Hills shortly after he arrived in L.A. from Kentucky. "I got some cash," he said. "Believe me, it's a lot harder to make those decisions when you're broke. It's not so honorable when you've got a little money saved up and you've got a villa in Italy."[16]

Fresh off his triumph in *Good Night, and Good Luck*, Clooney's next film—another "passion project" with the same goal of starting provocative political conversation—opened, nearly a year after he'd filmed it. *Syriana* is loosely based on a book written by former CIA agent Robert Baer about corruption in the oil industry. It was another movie with which Clooney proved he wasn't afraid to alienate his fans by revealing his liberal politics, another movie that many said wouldn't have been made without Clooney's clout.

"I felt that we were sticking our necks out," Clooney said, "but these films were not designed to make money. Everything else is icing . . . You've got to stick with your convictions, do what you want to do and hope that it strikes a chord. That you can't control. We couldn't have done *Good Night, and Good Luck* without doing *Unscripted* and *K Street*. At least we're living or dying on our own taste."[17]

Syriana was written and directed by Stephen Gaghan, who had won an Oscar for writing *Traffic*. Before the film came out, Gaghan knew *Syriana* could get them in trouble. "But it's good trouble," he said. "It's raising debate, it's bringing up issues, and talking about them, much in the same way that *Three Kings* did, four or five years after the fact of the first Gulf War. This movie aims to actually put a face on enemies, and say let's discover how these actually happen. Which is always dangerous, because people get mad."[18]

Clooney plays a character based on the 53-year-old Baer. Veteran CIA agent Bob Barnes is a government-paid assassin whose target is a prince who is heir to the throne of an oil-rich Persian Gulf country. Barnes follows orders because he believes he is acting for the good of his country.

Clooney is a supporting actor in the film. Though "his screen time is limited, Clooney serves as an anchor for *Syriana*, an ambitious political thriller about oil-industry corruption that overloads the viewer with information before paying off in an exciting, illuminating third act," wrote Carla Meyer of the *Sacramento Bee*.[19]

The success of both *Good Night, and Good Luck* and *Syriana* reflected the heightened political awareness of the times and satisfied the public's increased interest in political films.[20] They also may have whetted Clooney's appetite for getting more involved in world events.

To play Barnes, Clooney gained 30 pounds in just the 30 days he had between wrapping *Ocean's Twelve* and beginning work on *Syriana*. The "depressing" weight gain was necessary, Clooney said: "I needed to feel like I looked and seemed like somebody completely different than somebody who's instantly recognizable," he said. Between the extra weight and a scruffy, grey beard, it worked. "I could walk around and be completely left alone."[21]

Many critics felt that his work in *Syriana* was the best performance[22] he had yet turned in, which is ironic considering he's almost unrecognizable in the film and that in his own life, he had chosen to pursue success by leaving his home town, where he was instantly recognizable because of his resemblance to his father.

"*Syriana* confirms what *Good Night, and Good Luck* suggested: That George Clooney was always a character actor in a heartthrob's body. Beneath the scrubs, the Frank Sinatra act and the Sexiest Man Alive mantle beats the heart of an unselfish ensemble performer."[23]

As the new year began, Clooney and Steven Soderbergh, who had directed six of Clooney's films, closed their production company, Section Eight. The decision was said to be one that had been more or less planned when they started, when they said that they wouldn't want to continue on if they wound up spending more time as administrators than as filmmakers.[24] That didn't mean Clooney wanted to stop producing, however.

"We're going to do a film, Steven and I, right after [closing Section Eight] just to show it's not a fight between us. It's simply our fear of losing touch with what it is we really want to do, which is to make films," Clooney told the *Cincinnati Enquirer*.[25]

Not long afterward, near-universal agreement brought Clooney the recognition he'd long hoped for. The recognition was overwhelming and touched every facet of his career. In January 2006, Clooney's two "passion projects" picked up six Golden Globe nominations, including three nominations for Clooney as producer, director, and cowriter of *GNGL* and a nomination for supporting actor for his work in *Syriana*. *Good Night, and Good Luck* was tied with *Match Point* and *The Producers* as the films with the second highest number of nominations that year; only *Brokeback Mountain*, which received seven nods, had more.

"If you had asked me last January when I was finishing *Syriana* and starting *Good Night, and Good Luck*, if both films would be critical successes and making money, I would have laughed you out of the room,"

Clooney said. "The nice thing is, if these films make money, we can make more of these films."[26] His cowriter, Grant Heslov, added, "We wanted a film that would create discussion, and this has."

Some of that discussion, inevitably, was about Clooney's heretofore uncelebrated articulate and serious side.

"He's a good bit more complex than people realized initially," said Mark Gill, president of Warner Independent Pictures, which released *Good Night, and Good Luck*. "First he was that guy on the TV show, then he was that charming movie star who was great at parties. Now he's revealing that he's always been the son of a TV newsman."[27]

NOTES

1. Anne Thompson, "George Clooney: More Than a Superstar—Clooney's Clout Takes Him in New Directions of Show Biz," *Cincinnati Post*, January 3, 2006, p. B1.

2. Chris Nashawaty, "The Last Great Movie Star," *Entertainment Weekly*, December 12, 2005, p. 44.

3. John Lippman, "George Clooney Makes History," *The Wall Street Journal*, September 9, 2005, p. W7.

4. Nashawaty, "The Last Great Movie Star."

5. Margaret A. McGurk, "Serious George," *Cincinnati Enquirer*, October 21, 2005, p. E1.

6. Ibid.

7. Nick Clooney, "One Tough Audience for Premiere," *Cincinnati Post*, September 26, 2005, p. B1.

8. Rick Bird, "George Clooney's Tribute to TV Journalism," *Cincinnati Post*, October 20, 2005, p. T12.

9. Carrie Rickey, "A Timely Tale of TV's Nascent Power," *Philadelphia Inquirer*, October 14, 2005, p. W4.

10. Bird, "George Clooney's Tribute to TV Journalism."

11. David Denby, "Storm Warnings," *The New Yorker*, 2008, p. 96.

12. Amy Biancolli, " 'Good Night, and Good Luck' Has Classic Look," *Houston Chronicle*, October 14, 2005, p. 3.

13. Rex Reed, "In Cold Capote," *New York Observer*, September 26, 2005, Culture section, p. 1.

14. *Ebert & Roeper*, October 8, 2005, syndicated.

15. McGurk, "Serious George."

16. Ibid.

17. Thompson, "George Clooney: More Than a Superstar."

18. McGurk, "Serious George."

19. Carla Meyer, "Ambitious 'Syriana' Confuses Early but Finishes with a Bang," *Sacramento Bee*, December 9, 2005, p. TK26.

20. "Oscar Nominations Acknowledge Clooney's Range," *Cincinnati Post*, February 1, 2006, p. C3.

21. Jenelle Riley, "Charismatic, Clooney Relies on More Than That," *Ventura County Star*, December 9, 2005, Life, Arts & Living, p. 4.

22. Ibid.

23. Meyer, "Ambitious 'Syriana' Confuses Early but Finishes with a Bang."

24. McGurk, "Serious George."

25. Ibid.

26. Thompson, "George Clooney: More Than a Superstar."

27. Ibid.

Chapter 11

"ACADEMY AWARD WINNER GEORGE CLOONEY"

As 2006 began, George Clooney's life improved immeasurably from the previous year, when he was recuperating from the back injury suffered during the filming of *Syriana*. His latest movies were projects in which he'd invested both his money and his heart, and both had paid off—in profits and reception. Then, each was nominated for several Golden Globe awards.

To top it off, his father—a movie expert and that guy who'd tried his darndest to keep George from moving to Hollywood to become an actor ("I was afraid that even with talent he wouldn't be able to break through and succeed. What I shortchanged him on was his absolute dedication," he said in 1997)[1]—began researching to confirm what he believed: that his son had set a record in Golden Globe nomination history. In fact, he couldn't find another person who had ever been nominated four times in the same year for all four facets of movie making: writing, directing, producing and acting.[2]

The oft-repeated prediction was that 2006, coming right after Clooney's worst year, would be the one he'd always remember because of the good things that would happen, starting January 31, when the Oscar nominations were announced.[3] Even more prescient was *Cincinnati Enquirer* reporter Margaret A. McGurk, who, three months before the Academy Award nominations were announced, wrote these words in a story about *Good Night, and Good Luck*: "George Clooney has been asked many times to present an Oscar. He always said no. His stock response: 'I'll go when I'm nominated.' This could be the year."[4]

Truer words were never written.

On February 1, every newspaper in the country could confirm McGurk's prediction and go it two better. Clooney was nominated for three Academy Awards: for best supporting actor in *Syriana*; for best director for *Good Night, and Good Luck*; and for original screenplay (with Grant Heslov) for *Good Night, and Good Luck*. *Good Night, and Good Luck*, the movie that would never have been made but for Clooney (though he was not officially credited as producer) was also nominated for best picture, best cinematography, and best art direction—a total of seven nominations in all.

Clooney heard the news while watching the Oscar nomination show on E!, a cable television station.[5] Nick and Nina heard the news on TV that morning, as well. Having waited, palms sweating, they then began making phone calls. Their family and friends were much more excited than the honored man himself.[6]

Most people who had arrived in Hollywood the way George had, who had climbed the rungs of the ladder in the slow but steady way he had and who had endured canceled pilots, unreleased films, and bad reviews the way he had, would probably be understandably thrilled and overwhelmed at the amazing news. George, however, simply planned to fly to Cabo San Lucas (where he was headed to shoot a coffee commercial "to pay for the last couple of years") and have a drink to toast his success.[7] (Clooney, by the way, has starred in countless commercials over the years—he has done ads for Martini & Rossi that run only in Italy, as well as commercials for Dolce & Gabbana, among others, and has done voiceovers for many more companies, including Budweiser and AT&T.)

Clooney also joked, "We'll be able to say six nominations for *Good Night, and Good Luck*. That'll look good on the DVD box. I think what awards are really about is a way to get more people to see movies like this."

This time, Nick didn't have to do the research—it was the first time anyone had been nominated for acting in and directing two different movies. But he did it, anyway.[8]

Perhaps it doesn't need to be said that Nick was proud of his son. George had to be pleased. But he kept up his self-effacing demeanor. In typical deadpan style, he told reporters at Berlin's annual film festival, where *Syriana* was screened, "I don't think we're going to win any. There's been a lot of *Brokeback Mountain* stuff." But, he admitted, "Oscar nominations are as important as anything. The hope is that people will see this film—I don't know about wins."[9]

Nevertheless, Clooney was considered a frontrunner for the best supporting actor award.[10] He was a guest on the *Barbara Walters' 25th Oscar Special* (during which Walters gushed, "You are so handsome!")—just one of the countless high-profile places Clooney's face was plastered in wake of the nominations. The *Cincinnati Post* asked Nick Clooney whether even he was tired of seeing his son. "What I'm tired of is getting the phone calls that say, 'Now, I need six more pictures of him when he was 12.' We are getting depleted," Nick said.[11]

Nick had been to several Academy Awards presentations as a reporter in L.A. in the 1980s, but his son had never attended. George almost went in 2002, when *O Brother, Where Art Thou?* was nominated for best screenplay, but he decided to wait until he was nominated. "That's when I belong on that stage. You have to earn that."[12]

So he earned it in grand style, with three nominations and, on March 5, 2006, one golden Oscar. On the red carpet before the ceremony, Clooney told reporters he wasn't nervous. "That worries me more than anything," he said of his lack of butterflies.[13]

When asked whether he had a preference about winning for one film or the other, he said, "Well, it's funny, because we've been rather unburdened by success at these awards shows, so we're pretty good at losing—so I'm not really very concerned with winning so much. I'll be the [guy] in the back."[14]

Quite the opposite. Clooney was all over the ceremony, from beginning to end. "If he wasn't on the red carpet giving generous time to the press, he was taking part in host Jon Stewart's opening sketch or he was being mentioned in someone else's acceptance speech," according to the *Cincinnati Post*'s staff and wire reports.[15]

Howard Berger, cowinner for makeup for *The Chronicles of Narnia*, said in his acceptance speech, "Well, I'm just glad that Clooney doesn't do makeup."

Accepting the award for best documentary short, Corinne Marrinan thanked her family, HBO, and the Academy—for sitting her next to Clooney at the nominees' luncheon.

Then, George Clooney received his first Academy Award, for best supporting actor in *Syriana*. Winning for this particular nomination meant the most to him in view of everything he had gone through to get the role.[16]

When Clooney's moment arrived, here's what he said:

"Wow—. Wow—. All right, so I'm not winning [best] director," he joked.

"It's a funny thing about winning an Academy Award, this will always be sort of synonymous with your name from here on. Oscar-winner George Clooney, sexiest man alive 1997, Batman, died today in a freak accident. . . ."

But then Clooney turned serious: "Listen, I don't quite know how you compare art. You look at these performances this year of these actors—unless we all did the same role—everyone put on bat suits and we'll try that—unless we all did the same role, I don't know how you compare it. They are stellar performances and wonderful work and I am honored, truly honored to be up here. . . . And finally, I would say that you know we are a little bit out of touch every now and then here in Hollywood—every once in a while—and I think that's probably a good thing. We're the ones to talk about AIDS when it was just being whispered. And we talked about civil rights when it wasn't really popular. You know we bring up subjects. We're the ones, you know, this Academy gave Hattie McDaniel an Oscar in 1939 when blacks were still sitting in the backs of theaters."

He concluded, "I'm proud to be part of this Academy, proud to be part of this community and proud to be 'out of touch'—and I thank you so much for this."[17]

As he predicted, Clooney later lost in the directing and screenplay categories for *Good Night, and Good Luck*. The Oscar for best picture went to *Crash*.

Still, the post-Oscar Clooneyfest continued almost at the rate of the pre-Oscar Clooneyfest. A story in the *Daily News of Los Angeles* was bylined "Daily News Women Staff Writers" and headlined, "Why Do We Love George Clooney?"[18]

Some of their reasons:

"He looks mighty fine in a tux. Even if it's the same one from Armani that he's admitted to wearing for the last 10 years. He said he thought about going out Sunday to get a new tux, 'or I could play basketball with my friends' . . . so he wore the same tux."

"He's good for a snappy comeback. 'Who else do you like here tonight?' Roger Ebert asked him Sunday. 'I don't like anybody else here,' he told Ebert on the red carpet. 'You know that Ang Lee character [who was also nominated in the best director category]? I don't like him. I think he's a Communist.'"

"He's an old-fashioned movie star: Like Cary Grant and Clark Gable, fans love him. When he stepped on the red carpet Sunday night, a big cheer went up from the bleachers."

Ah, yes, his public. Not only was Clooney's popularity nearly universal among the press, but both men and women in the greater audience seemed to admire him, as well.

"This year the Oscars might as well have been called the Georges. He was the center of attention all night. . . . Fans and well-wishers wouldn't leave him alone en route to the Governors Ball, and when he got there, the crowd gave him a round of applause. But Clooney wasn't just on the receiving end of all that goodwill. 'The highlight was after winning,' he said, when he saw Robert Altman in the greenroom. 'I loved being able to sit down with Robert Altman for a minute and get him a Scotch. It was a good night.'"[19]

Days afterward, BBC News announced that the presenters' gift bag—which included a pocket computer, a designer kimono, and a pearl necklace—that had been given to George at the Academy Awards ceremony raised more than $45,000 when he offered it in an online auction, with the proceeds going to the United Way relief effort for the victims of the disastrous hurricanes that had hit the United States the preceding year. His publicist told the BBC that "it was common for him to offer such gifts to charity."[20]

Common gestures from him, perhaps. But that winter had been uncommonly good to George. Now his focus was going to shift toward doing even more good in the world.

NOTES

1. Lorrie Lynch, "Why George Clooney Says, 'I Live for the Moment,'" *USA Weekend*, September 26–28, 1997. http://www.usaweekend.com/97_issues/970 928/970928cov_clooney.html.

2. "A Good Year for George," *Cincinnati Post*, December 14, 2005, p. B14.

3. Ibid.

4. Margaret A. McGurk, "Serious George," *Cincinnati Enquirer*, October 21, 2005, p. 1E.

5. Giuliana DePandi, E! Entertainment Television, Los Angeles, January 31, 2006, PRNewswire.

6. Nick Clooney, "Reflecting on Oscar, Hard Times," *Cincinnati Post*, February 1, 2006, p. C1.

7. Oscar Nominations Acknowledge Clooney's Range," *Cincinnati Post*, February 1, 2006, p. C3.

8. Clooney, "Reflecting on Oscar, Hard Times."

9. "George: No Oscars for Me—Clooney Talks about (Not) Winning Awards . . . and Weight Gain," *Cincinnati Post*, February 13, 2006, p. C8.

10. Richard Corliss, "Place Your Bets," *Time*, February 27, 2006, p. 64.

11. Rick Bird, "George in L.A., Nick in N.Y.—And All Fingers Crossed," *Cincinnati Post*, March 3, 2006, p. C4.

12. Ibid.

13. Staff and wire reports, "Clooney a Big Hit at Oscars," *Cincinnati Post*, March 7, 2006, p. C1.

14 Ibid.

15. Ibid.

16. George Clooney, interviewed by Barbara Walters, *Barbara Walters' 25th Oscar Special*, broadcast on ABC-TV on March 1, 2006.

17. Transcript of Academy Award presentation.

18. Daily News Women Staff Writers, "By George . . . He Is One Sexy-Looking Hunk o' Man," *Daily News of Los Angeles*, March 6, 2006, p. U9.

19. "Man of the Hour: By George, Mr. Clooney Ruled the Oscars!" *People*, March 20, 2006, p. 139.

20. See http://news.bbc.co.uk/2/hi/entertainment/4859832.stm.

Chapter 12

MESSENGER OF PEACE

Auctioning off his gift bags is but a small, telling part of George Clooney. He is prone to acts of charity, true, but he is also an activist and
even was named a United Nations Messenger of Peace.

As early as 1992, two years before *ER*, reporters who knew him were
writing about this side of the actor. "Despite his reputation as something of a party animal in Hollywood, Clooney exhibited a serious side
when he talked about the Los Angeles riots touched off by the not-
guilty verdicts in the Rodney King case," wrote Greg Paeth.[1]

Clooney explained that it was partly his upbringing that prompted
him to do something that night. "We went down Thursday night,
which was the worst night to go down, to try and put out some fires.
And then we realized they were still making the fires at the time, so we
left, and then Friday, Saturday and Sunday we were in Watts—the real
war zone—cleaning up and putting out fires."

Clooney had another explanation for why he and some friends drove
to South Central L.A. to help. "It was Irish Catholic guilt—you have
a responsibility to other people in the world. Everybody was leaving
town, and I said this is not the time to be leaving," he said. Clooney's
experience that weekend was a turning point for him, a time when

he realized the difference between talking about politics and getting involved in making the world a better place.[2]

The election of George W. Bush in 2000 might also have sparked Clooney to become more politically active[3]; by December 2001, the press was regularly calling him an "activist." The first time this occurred was in a report on his role in organizing a celebrity telethon, "A Tribute to Heroes," for victims of the September 11 terrorist attacks.[4] "Clooney, 40, has emerged as Tinseltown's BMOC, a guy who uses his growing clout to support projects and causes he believes in," wrote Clarissa Cruz in *Entertainment Weekly*.[5]

Proving the cliché that "no good deed goes unpunished," Clooney's role in that charity led to some public back and forth with Fox News commentator Bill O'Reilly, who blasted Clooney and his friends and claimed that the money raised through the telethon was slow in getting to victims. Clooney vehemently denied the accusation, saying the money quickly was distributed to those who needed it.

Two years later, Clooney spoke out against the invasion of Iraq. The response to his position from the political right (supporters of the war put him in a deck of "weasel" playing cards) angered him greatly, and some of the resentment went into making *Good Night, and Good Luck*.[6]

Just before the invasion of Iraq began, there was debate about whether it was unpatriotic for celebrities to comment about the possibility of war. Clooney was one of 100 Hollywood celebrities who signed a letter asking President Bush not to attack Iraq. In response to the letter, a flyer was distributed to talent agencies and production companies in Hollywood, calling every person who signed the letter a "traitor." In what had to remind Clooney of McCarthyism, the flyer had been created and sent by a group supporting the invasion of Iraq.[7]

Clooney's next high-profile humanitarian effort came two years later, as he helped to plan another telethon, this time to raise money for those hurt by the tsunami in Asia. Bill O'Reilly, of Fox's *The O'Reilly Factor*, blasted Clooney yet again. "You may also remember that Clooney strenuously objected to *The Factor* investigation that uncovered problems in distributing the 9/11 money, even though we proved our case and the Red Cross revamped its entire operation because of it," O'Reilly said.[8]

Never one to back down from a fight, Clooney responded with a letter released by his publicist: "It is incumbent upon me to help you get your facts straight. First, to clarify, it was not the Red Cross but the United Way that sponsored that telethon . . . an easy mistake to make . . . if you're 3."

Clooney continued: "Second, contrary to what you claim, no one objected to you investigating where the funds were going, but we strenuously objected to you insinuating that it was a fraud (which is what you did) as we were still waiting for a list of names of the dead."[9]

Clooney closed his letter by personally inviting O'Reilly to take part in the telethon. Bill O'Reilly answered Clooney's comments and invitation in a newspaper story. "Even in the United States where the government is supposed to oversee the charity business, problems abound. The United Way recently had a huge scandal in Washington, D.C. And according to its own chapter in Bergen Country, New Jersey, the United Way screwed up big time in the first few months after 9/11, even if Clooney won't admit it," he wrote.

"So now Clooney and other stars are asking for money again. In a great public relations stroke, he even asked me to be a part of the tsunami telethon. His invitation stated, 'Mr. O'Reilly, either you ante up and help out and be that watchdog that you feel we clearly need, or you stand on the sidelines and cast stones.'"

O'Reilly concluded, "Because the telethon donations are all going to the American Red Cross, I have agreed to help the cause. The ARC is now transparent and accountable, and I respect the changes its leadership has put in place since 9/11. Whether all the money the telethon raised will really help the tsunami victims, I can't say. But generosity is its own reward, and if we can help, we should. Nothing in life is guaranteed, but Americans have always helped the downtrodden and continuing the tradition is worthy."[10]

Clooney's interest in politics was surprising to some. Whether his serious political side had taken time to develop or had been suppressed while Clooney tried to become a success in his career, it emerged and became increasingly evident around the time his success took off. One particular pet peeve was Clooney's indignation over being called a "liberal," as if the word itself were some sort of insult. He began trying, in his own way, to restore the honorable meaning to the word.[11]

"It blows my mind," Clooney said. "Because [unlike conservatives] we don't have to put the word 'compassionate' in front of it to say we actually [care] about people. I'm going to keep saying 'liberal' as loud as I can and as often as I can."[12]

He realized he was straddling two different worlds as he worked for various causes while enjoying his privileged lifestyle. "I'm in this weird place: I have this beautiful house in Italy and I have these social agendas. I don't want to give up that lifestyle because I enjoy it, but I also feel that I have a responsibility. So the way I try to rationalize that, and it may just be Irish-Catholic guilt, is, for instance, with this casino [in Las Vegas, planned with Rande Gerber] 25 percent of anything it makes will go to the Make Poverty History campaign. It's the only way I can reconcile being successful."[13]

Clooney's willingness to get involved in causes hit closer to home in 2007 during the Writers Guild of America strike in Hollywood. Clooney unofficially tried to help settle that strike and reportedly also donated money to the Guild to help the out-of-work writers.[14] Ironically, months later, the Writers Guild rejected Clooney's request for a writing credit for his movie *Leatherheads*, and Clooney quit the Guild in protest. He had sought a writing credit along with his directing, producing, and starring roles in the film, saying in news service reports that he personally had given "the languishing 17-year-old project a major overhaul" and "felt he had written all but two of the scenes." The request was voted down, 2–1.[15]

Once the writer's strike was settled, there was some concern that the Screen Actors Guild might strike as well, giving the film and television industry a 1–2 punch it didn't need. Clooney, along with Tom Hanks, met with SAG President Alan Rosenberg to suggest that he start negotiating early to avoid problems before the June 30 contract expiration.[16]

"During a two-hour meeting Tuesday night, Clooney and Hanks— joined by actors Sally Field and Rob Lowe—urged Rosenberg and guild negotiator Doug Allen to tone down their rhetoric and get to the bargaining table, according to anonymous reports," the *Los Angeles Times* reported.[17]

The session was called after Clooney, Hanks, Robert De Niro, and Meryl Streep took out a full-page ad in the Hollywood trade papers asking the Guild to begin negotiations. As the contract expiration date approached, Clooney got involved again, urging members of two unions to stop arguing. He released a two-page letter addressing the dispute between the American Federation of Television and Radio Artists (AFTRA) and the Screen Actors Guild (SAG), writing, "What we can't do is pit artist against artist."

Some stars were petitioning members of AFTRA to ratify their tentative agreement with the studios, but others asked AFTRA to push for a better deal while SAG continued negotiations. Clooney called the fight counterproductive "[b]ecause the one thing you can be sure of is that stories about Jack Nicholson vs. Tom Hanks only strengthens the negotiating power" of the studios.[18] Clooney also called on higher-paid actors to chip in a greater share of union dues and for 10 A-listers, including Nicholson and Hanks, to sit down with studio heads once a year to adjust pay for actors.

Once his own world was right, Clooney went on to the larger world, addressing the ongoing genocide in Darfur, a region in western Sudan. He first was alerted to the situation after reading columns written by Nicholas Kristof in the *New York Times*, he said.[19] Shortly after his father's failed congressional race, early in 2006, the pair discussed the idea of a trip there. "We knew great reporters had done terrific stories, but the story wasn't getting any traction," Nick said. "George said to me, 'Why don't you go over and do something?' His thought was that we could do it together."[20]

Nick Clooney called a former State Department official to discuss the possibility. David Pressman, a human rights attorney and former aide to Secretary of State Madeline Albright, wanted to meet with George to verify the sincerity of his intentions.[21] Within weeks, Pressman and the Clooneys flew to Chad and then to Sudan.

After returning from his nine-day trip, Clooney spoke to the United Nations Security Council, pleading with its members to help stop the genocide in Darfur. The briefing was organized by the Ellie Wiesel Foundation for Humanity.[22] Describing Darfur as this century's first genocide, Clooney warned the Council that millions of Sudanese would die unless it took "real and effective measures before the end of the month to put an end to the killing and rapes in the war-torn region."[23] He also told the 15-member body that the way it dealt with the crisis there "will be your legacy, your Rwanda, your Cambodia, your Auschwitz."

Nobel Laureate and UN Messenger of Peace Elie Wiesel, who himself had survived that notorious Nazi death camp, reminded Council members that the UN Charter obligated them to save lives.

A documentary, *A Journey to Darfur*, produced by Nick and George Clooney after the trip, alerted viewers to something else: they had risked their lives to go. "There wasn't a minute I didn't think we were going to get killed," George Clooney said in the documentary, which aired on cable TV's AmericanLife network in January 2007. George and Nick hosted a screening of the film for a congressional delegation in Washington, D.C., and copies were also distributed to church groups and other organizations. Tapes created on the trip and eventually used for the documentary were confiscated twice during the visit—one reminder that the Clooneys were in a war zone. A second reminder was the fact they were accompanied by armed guards.[24]

Written and hosted by Nick Clooney, the documentary included interviews with refugees, both victims of and witnesses to the horrors taking place in the region. Nick also interviewed his son on film for the first time, and George spoke about what he had seen and how it affected him. The film was "both a primer on the genocide in the region and, more subtly, a reflection on the power and limits of celebrity. The film deftly walks a fine line of staying focused on the issue of Darfur, yet knowing one reason people watch and listen to the story about a far off region is because George is 'the sexiest man alive,'" said Rick Bird in the *Cincinnati Post*.[25]

In the documentary, George told of a little girl who tugged at his finger, asking when he would come back with help: "I said [through the translator], 'Tell her soon.' She giggled and pulled on my finger. I asked what she said. It was, 'That's what you always say.' I thought, man, has she seen us before. . . . The problem is we show up, we get on television and we raise a lot of Cain—and that little girl is every bit in as much danger today as she was five months ago."[26]

Obviously, the Clooneys wanted their trip to draw attention to the issues in Darfur, even timing their journey to happen just before a march and rally for Darfur in Washington, D.C. The blanket news coverage of their trip helped bring 50,000 people to a rally that had hoped to draw 5,000. Quite a success, or so it seemed.

"The very next day [after the rally] the President sent his No. 2 guy to Nigeria where the peace talks were under way and called the president of Sudan and told him to get back to the negotiations," Nick said.[27]

The first-ever agreement to allow a U.N. peacekeeping force to enter the region came in early May, but it didn't last long. "It still showed when the world keeps the pressure on, something can be done," Nick said. "When it turns its eyes away—well, it fell apart because we had the summer of Lebanon and Israel and that sucked all the oxygen out of the news cycle."[28]

His son criticized the U.S. news media, complaining that news outlets ignore the story because they underestimate interest in such atrocities.[29] "The U.S. press took such a pass on the Bush administration that they are as responsible for us marching into Iraq as the administration. There is no question about it. They were afraid to be marked as unpatriotic," he said.[30]

After George's appearance at the U.N. Security Council, he also visited Egypt and China to discuss Darfur with leaders there. The dire situation in Darfur continued, and Clooney did not forget what he'd seen there. In 2007, he joined with colleagues from the *Ocean's* films, Pressman, producer Jerry Weintraub, and actors Brad Pitt, Matt Damon, and Don Cheadle, to form a nonprofit organization, Not on Our Watch, to raise money for the 2.5 million civilians in Darfur who had fled their homes.

The group organized benefit screenings of *Ocean's Thirteen* to raise funds for their organization and for the International Rescue Committee. The cast itself donated $5.5 million. When *Ocean's Thirteen* premiered at the Cannes Film Festival, NOOW raised a total of $9.3 million in one night through donations.

"There are only a few things we can do—protect them where we can, and provide food, water, health care, and counseling," George Clooney told the press. "We're just trying to get them to live long enough to get to the next step."[31]

Though Clooney's efforts to help Darfur got a lot of press, some of his charitable efforts did not. In June 2007, for example, he offered

himself as an escort at a movie premiere to the highest bidder in an
online auction to benefit Realizing the Dream, an organization run by
Martin Luther King III with the goal of ending poverty in America.

George's interest in philanthropic activities was a family tradition he
grew up with, his mother said.[32] "We were always doing events for char-
ities and certainly at Christmas time, there were several families that
we would hear from, and we'd go out and buy presents for them," Nina
recalled. "We involved our kids in what we were doing, although some
of it may have been not having a babysitter to leave them with!"

Unfettered by the need for babysitters but with the knowledge that
the fame he'd won could help him help others, George Clooney was
able to travel the world. One reason he could do so was that he was
invited to become a U.N. Messenger of Peace.

The designation of Messengers of Peace is given at the discretion
of the Secretary General of the United Nations, a peacekeeping official said. The U.N. has 10 Messengers of Peace, including Yo-Yo Ma
and Jane Goodall, selected from the fields of art, literature, music, and
sports. It is a title that has been around for decades and that is bestowed
on "global citizens" for an initial period of three years. Recipients are
prominent personalities who volunteer their time, talent, and passion
to raise awareness of the U.N.'s efforts.

Messengers of Peace are selected because of their interests, their
related work, and their ability to serve as advocates for the United
Nations. The designation is an official appointment, has no pay, and
has few specific duties. Clooney is the first Messenger of Peace to be
appointed with a special responsibility for U.N. peacekeeping. He was
chosen because he had shown an interest over several years in a specific
conflict, but he also spoke out on similar issues.

In January 2008, after accepting the honor, he returned to Darfur as
part of a tour planned by Jane Holl Lute, a U.N. peacekeeping official.
The 15-day trip was a physically and emotionally difficult voyage to
various places in Sudan, Chad, the Democratic Republic of the Congo,
and India.[33] Three days after Clooney left Chad, rebels killed hundreds
at his hotel.

After that tense trip, which included a scary helicopter ride out of
N'Djamena, Chad, in a sandstorm, Clooney suffered from a case of ma-
laria and from a lingering disappointment: "I've been very depressed

since I got back. I'm terrified that it isn't in any way helping. That bringing attention can cause more damage. You dig a well or build a health-care facility and they're a target for somebody. A lot more people know about Darfur, but absolutely nothing is different. Absolutely nothing."[34]

Nick Birnback, a U.N. Department of Peacekeeping official who traveled with Clooney, praised him as a practical person. "He's very operationally minded. He's not a sort of hug-the-kids, why-can't-we-all-get-along, sing-*Kumbaya* person. You need helicopters? Let's get you helicopters. You need help? What do you want me to do? That optic is something we're very comfortable with because we're operational—we're the part of the U.N. that goes and does things. He's a logical person to work with."[35]

When asked to compare Clooney's actual involvement in the U.N. with its other peace messengers, Birnback declined but said, "We are absolutely thrilled to have him on board. He has been very generous to us with his time, and he recorded a public service announcement for us. We need his time and his engagement and we're lucky to have him."

Many who traveled with Clooney on that trip were surprised by how committed and engaged he was. They were impressed not only by his dedication but by his intellect and his attention to the subject. "This is a guy who does his homework, who has a command of the subject matter in a way you wouldn't dare to expect from a celebrity endorsement guy. If you watch the PSA, you'll get a sense of his take on things. He's very self-deprecating—his approach is like that," Birnback said.

Clooney's interest in the wider world, he told his fellow travelers, came from his father's job as a newsman. "He knows a great deal about what's going on, and he's using his star power for the greater good. It's quite inspiring."

After the trip, Clooney filmed a public service announcement for the United Nations Department of Peacekeeping Officials. The PSA message came from Clooney, the official said. "Peace Is Hard," which can be viewed at www.betterworldcampaign.org or http://www.you-tube.com/unbluehelmets, was filmed as part of the 50th anniversary of peacekeeping and was shown on television all over the world.

"Peace is not just a colored ribbon. It's more than a wristband or a t-shirt. It's not just a donation or a 5K race. It's not just a folk song . . .

or a white dove . . . and peace is certainly more than . . . a celebrity endorsement. Peace is a fulltime job. It's protecting civilians, overseeing elections and disarming ex-combatants. . . . The U.N. has more than 100,000 peacekeepers on the ground in places others can't or won't go, doing things others can't or won't do. Peace, like war, must be waged."

This TV job, though it brings less pay, is perhaps even more important—and is certainly more telling—than his five years on *ER*. But it's because of *ER* that he can be effective at it.

NOTES

1. Greg Paeth, "George Clooney's Latest Series Given New Life," *Cincinnati Post*, July 21, 1992, p. 1B.

2. Ian Parker, "Somebody Has to Be in Control," *New Yorker*, April 14, 2008. p. 40.

3. Ibid.

4. John Horn, "George Clooney Rolls the Dice—The 'Ocean's Eleven' Star Continues Running Hollywood's Table. Now He's Cashing in His Chips to Do What He Really Wants," *Newsweek*, December 17, 2001, p. 64.

5. Clarissa Cruz, "By George He's Got It—The Ocean's Eleven Star Proves He's Head of the Hollywood Class," *Entertainment Weekly*, December 14, 2001, p. 10.

6. Parker, "Somebody Has to Be in Control."

7. Nick Madigan, "Oscar Show Goes on, but Mood Is Subdued by the Fighting in Iraq," *New York Times*, March 24, 2003, p. E5.

8. Sharon Cotliar and Stephen M. Silverman, "George Clooney Bites Back at Bill O'Reilly," *People.com*, January 11, 2005, http://www.people.com/people/article/0,,1016211,00.html.

9. Letter from Stan Rosenfield, as quoted by People.com, January 11, 2005, http://www.people.com/people/article/0,,1016211,00.html.

10. Cotliar and Silverman, "George Clooney Bites Back at Bill O'Reilly."

11. David Ansen, "Curious George—Everything You Thought You Knew about Clooney—The Roguish Guy's Guy and Lady-Killer—Is True. So How'd He direct One of the Best and Smartest Movies of the Year?" *Newsweek*, October 10, 2005, p. 60.

12. Ibid.

13. Ibid.

14. Ibid.

15. Karla Peterson, "Public Eye," *San Diego Union-Tribune*, April 5, 2008, p. A2.

16. Richard Verrier, "Stars Bring Muscle to Actors Guild Talks," *Los Angeles Times*, February 22, 2008, Financial.

17. Ibid.

18. Ryan Nakashima, "George Clooney Urges Unity among Actors," *Ventura County Star*, June 27, 2008, Business.

19. Parker, "Somebody Has to Be in Control."

20. Gail H. Towns, "An Interview with Nick Clooney," *Cincinnati Parent*, September 1, 2007.

21. Parker, "Somebody Has to Be in Control."

22. UN press release, http://www.un.org/apps/news/story.asp?NewsID=198 44&Cr=sudan&Cr1=Dafur&Kw1=clooney&Kw2=&Kw3=.

23. UN press release, http://www.un.org/apps/news/story.asp?NewsID=198 44&Cr=sudan&Cr1=Dafur&Kw1=clooney&Kw2=&Kw3=.

24. Rick Bird, "Nick, George Documentary Tells Darfur Experiences," *Cincinnati Post*, January 11, 2007, p. B1.

25. Ibid.

26. Ibid.

27. Ibid.

28. Ibid.

29. Ginanne Brownell, "The Last Word: George Clooney; The Frustrated American," *Newsweek International*, February 12, 2007.

30. Ibid.

31. "'Ocean's 13' Cast Donates $5.5M for Darfur," *Cincinnati Post*, June 28, 2007, p. C10.

32. Towns, "An Interview with Nick Clooney."

33. Parker, "Somebody Has to Be in Control."

34. Joel Stein, "Guess Who Came to Dinner?" *Time*, March 3, 2008, p. 46.

35. All references to the U.N. peacekeeping official are the result of a phone interview with Nick Birnback with the author on October 30, 2008.

Chapter 13

BECOMING PAUL NEWMAN

In between efforts to help the world, George Clooney was busy working, but he continued on his path of choosing the unexpected and going the extra mile both in work and in his day-to-day life.

While in Tobaccoville, North Carolina, in 2007, filming *Leatherheads*, Clooney made news for—what else?—being the good guy, brightening the day for a bunch of local kids and their mom.

The kids, 10-year-old Carter Fontaine and his 6- and 5-year-old brothers, Chandler and Chase, set up a lemonade stand during their spring break near their home, which was also near Clooney's movie set. Selling lemonade for 25 cents, they figured they'd make a few dollars. They probably didn't realize they'd make a new friend.

Clooney heard about the stand and went over to buy a cup of lemonade. The boys' mother, Courtney, offered him a free one, but he insisted on paying—sending someone over with a $20 bill and refusing to take any change. Not bad. But the best part came when Clooney agreed to pose for a photo with Courtney and some of her friends.[1]

Clooney's personal life made news later that year, as well. It could be said that news of his newest girlfriend made quite an impact.

"Clooney suffered a broken rib and some scrapes when the motor-cycle he and a friend were riding collided with a car as the actor tried to pass the other vehicle, authorities said," the *Cincinnati Post* reported.[2]

The accident happened near Manhattan, in New Jersey, and intro-duced the name "Sarah Larson" to Clooney fans. Larson suffered a bro-ken toe, but it was reported that the couple was each wearing a helmet at the time of the accident. Reports said the pair met while Larson was waitressing at a Las Vegas club.

The premiere of *Michael Clayton* a few days later gave Clooney and Larson a chance to show off their injuries in public, whether they wanted to or not. "If his torso were a classic pop tune, it would be somewhere between *Deep Purple* and *Somewhere over the Rainbow*. His cracked rib and severe abrasions will get his full attention for some time to come, but he was back at work the next day," his father wrote in his column. "His friend Sarah may have gotten the worst of it. She has a broken toe and all the other toes are sprained. I dubbed her 'Princess Purple Toe,' and no one looks better on crutches than she."[3]

Nick also noted that "George got little sympathy from his friends. When we went to his hotel room, we saw a tiny tricycle in the corner. It was a gift from his friend Renee Zellweger. I will leave to your imagi-nation the accompanying note."

Clooney presumably got many more notes soon afterward as he was nominated for his first best actor Oscar for *Michael Clayton*. The nom-ination capped off what the Associated Press writer David Germain called "a post-*Batman* decade of wild success on far-flung projects as an actor, writer, director, and producer, sometimes handling all four jobs at once. . . . After years of taking what was offered, including bad movies such as *Batman & Robin*, Clooney took charge of his career. The result has left the former star of TV's *ER* an Academy-Award-winning actor and Oscar-nominated filmmaker who uses his stardom to do films he truly cares about, including the new legal drama, *Michael Clayton*."[4]

Germain concluded, "Even his failures look noble. Soderbergh di-rected Clooney in two ambitious duds, the science-fiction saga *Solaris* and last year's film-noir throwback *The Good German*. Yet both earned them admiration for the effort when they simply could have made an-other formulaic Hollywood yarn."[5]

With *Michael Clayton*, Clooney took a starring role in a film he believed in, a film about a former prosecutor who works in a New York City law firm making problems go away for wealthy clients. The charming, middle-aged, formerly successful character must learn to grapple with failure.

"It's not hard for George to envision if the road had turned the other way," said *Michael Clayton* writer-director Tony Gilroy, who felt that an actor who succeeded at an early age would be unable to get at the core of this character. "There's something infinitely more sad about someone who you really feel has squandered everything. Here's a guy who has skated on his looks and skated on his charms, and you realize he's completely lost. He was perfect for that."[6]

Clooney worked with co-star Tilda Swinton on the film and then again on another movie, *Burn after Reading*, which also starred *Ocean's Eleven* pal Brad Pitt. Clooney often works with actors he has enjoyed working with previously, both because he enjoys working with people he likes and because he is now so famous he prefers working with people who aren't intimidated by him and who participate in his joking banter.[7]

"There's a bunch of actors who can be really good in a film, but they will make everyone suffer, or the director suffer, because it becomes about them. Some of them thrive in this world where things have to be going wrong, other people have to be unhappy, for you to get your performance out. When you find people who aren't like that, you tend to like to work with them," Clooney told the Associated Press.[8]

In 2007 and 2008, Clooney's movies included *Michael Clayton*, *Leatherheads*, and *Burn after Reading*. Reflecting on the long string of movies he'd made in a relatively short period of time, he often acknowledged that his marathon moviemaking wasn't simply the result of being a workaholic but was a product of his keen awareness that his time could end.

"My aunt Rosemary was the biggest star on Earth, and then she was a flop because rock 'n' roll came in and pop music went out. She didn't become less of a singer. In fact, she became a better singer, but it didn't matter. Things change. So understanding that is a really important element to what it is I do," he said.

"I'm going to force people to make films they don't want to make. Believe me, no one's encouraging us to make *Good Night, and Good Luck* or *Syriana* or *The Good German* or *Solaris*. . . . To me, the idea is there's a period of time that I have where I'm able to force-feed films down people's throats, and I don't know how long that lasts. So I've been sort of on a mad rush to try and slam films down that I'd like to see made."[9]

He did manage to find time for relationships, including the one with Sarah Larson. He created a stir in February 2008 when he brought her to the Academy Awards, the first time Clooney had brought a girl-friend to the Oscars ceremony—and the first time he'd been nomi-nated as best actor.

"As the two moved slowly down the red carpet Sunday night, the 46-year-old actor kept his hand on the small of Sarah Larson's back, rubbing her reassuringly as he talked to the press. The *Michael Clayton* star—who was up for Best Actor—was full of praise for his 28-year-old date, who looked radiant in a clingy floral Valentino gown," reported *People.com*.[10]

"She looks good, huh?" he said on the red carpet. He jokingly added, "I tried it on first and it looked terrible on me."

When she noted that the dress was "really heavy," he gallantly vol-unteered, "I will carry her."

Things weren't quite as happy inside during the ceremony, where Clooney lost the Oscar to Daniel Day-Lewis. But Clooney was a pres-ence at the ceremony, starting when he introduced the montage "80 years of Oscar."[11] He was introduced, as he once joked, as "Academy Award winner and nominee tonight George Clooney!"

"For the past eight decades, we've gathered each year to honor the outstanding achievements of filmmaking around the world. What started as an intimate dinner for a handful at a party at the Hollywood Roosevelt Hotel has grown in size and stature to include a worldwide audience numbering in the hundreds of millions."

As Clooney spoke the presumably scripted words, he didn't seem his comfortable self. But he warmed up.

"Eighty years of memories—a streaker running behind David Niven, Charlie Chaplin returning after years of exile, surprise winners, grand production numbers. Some great moments, some mistakes. But the one thing that has always been consistent . . . "

Pause. An ad lib? Maybe.

"It's long. [Lots of laughter.] No . . . it's unpredictable. Here's 80 years of Oscar."

That wasn't Clooney's only Oscar moment that night. When his *Michael Clayton* costar Tilda Swinton won the Oscar for best supporting actress, she took part of her short speech to tease Clooney.

"George Clooney! You know, the seriousness and the dedication to your art . . . seeing you climb into that rubber Batsuit from *Batman & Robin*—the one with the nipples, every morning under your costume— on the set, off the set—hanging upside down at lunch. You rock, man!"

The camera caught Clooney's hearty laughter.

Weeks later, the "best actor" loss must have been all but forgotten as the photo on the cover of the March 3 issue of *Time* wasn't Day-Lewis's but Clooney's.

Under the headline "The Last Movie Star," *Time* quoted Clooney's friend and partner in Smoke House productions Grant Heslov: "he's a throwback to what movie stars used to be."

"His strategy for being a movie star is pretty simple, if counterintuitive," Joel Stein wrote. "He makes fun of himself."[12]

No other star, wrote Stein, "wears his celebrity so easily."

The headline's label fit perfectly at Clooney's next event, when he continued a family tradition by opening one of his movies at "home" in Maysville, Kentucky, about 60 miles southeast of Cincinnati, where his family members have lived for 100 years and where his father and aunt Rosemary grew up. When he was a kid in nearby Augusta, Maysville was the "big city" to George.

In March 2008, George was the superstar in Maysville. Fifty-five years after his aunt debuted her film *The Stars Are Singing* in Maysville, George brought *Leatherheads* there. He had always wanted to have a premiere in Maysville, but he needed the right film to bring to the historic (circa 1850) Washington Opera House. *Leatherheads* worked because the small towns where football started after World War II—the subject of the romantic comedy—in some ways resembled Maysville.

"You have to have the proper film to do this," Clooney said. "We couldn't bring *Syriana* here. Since [*Leatherheads*] is a movie where they go on whistle-stop tours all the time [to play games], it seemed like the perfect place to come."[13]

It wasn't easy. He had to convince Universal Pictures to bring a screen, a projector, and a sound system to a theater that hadn't shown a movie since 1964. The company also brought red carpeting and a cadre of publicists.

Not only was it fun for Clooney to bring a movie to his hometown, but the movie itself was designed to be simply fun. Clooney rewrote a 15-year-old script for the comedy, though he was publicly annoyed when the Writers Guild of America did not award him a formal share of the writing credit.[14]

He chose to make a light film because he wanted to direct again and because he didn't want to get pigeonholed as someone who directs only "issues films" like *Good Night, and Good Luck* and *Syriana*, he told "The Movie Guy."[15] In the film, Clooney plays Dodge Connolly, a past-his-prime pro football star who recruits a college hotshot and World War I hero to save his team. The two end up at odds over the affections of a newspaperwoman (Renee Zellweger) who is doing a story on the young recruit (John Krasinski.)

As a director, Clooney described himself as "fun."[16] At least one cast member would wholeheartedly agree. "He joked around a lot and after every shot he'd have to run back to video village—where they keep the monitors—and watch what we'd just shot. Even though he was getting worn out after so much running back and forth, just before every shot he'd still run about 100 yards down the playing field, run back and shoot the scene so he'd be totally out of breath like his character was supposed to be," said Ezra Buzzington, who played a referee early in the film.[17]

Buzzington's character has an exchange with Clooney's character in which Clooney challenges the referee's abilities and the referee challenges him back. "I'd work with George again in a heartbeat if he wanted me to," said Buzzington. "He was such a pro and so good-natured, it was a thrill to be one-on-one with him. When we shot our dialogue, I kind of had to pinch myself. I just kept thinking, 'I'm acting opposite George Clooney!' It was a blast."

Buzzington hadn't met Clooney before the shoot, but he knew the cinematographer, Tom Sigel. When Sigel greeted Buzzington on the first day of the shoot, Clooney was there, too.

"I was a little nervous, because, hey, it's George Clooney after all," said Buzzington, mentioning Sigel's greeting. "George was standing right there and stuck out his hand and introduced himself. Yeah. Like I wouldn't recognize him."

Buzzington added, "The greats are always nice, without exception—and he was nicer than any of them. I've worked with some big stars—Edward Norton, Jim Carrey, William H. Macy—and, believe me, though they were all wonderful and giving and sweet, George trumped them all. He's just such a real guy. Very, very down to earth and clearly grateful for the breaks he's been given in his career. And it shows."

The thousands of people who vied for tickets for the *Leatherheads* showing in Maysville would agree, particularly Blanche Chambers, a childhood friend of Rosemary Clooney's whose home was just blocks from the Opera House.

"George was always a cutup, but such a nice person," Chambers said. "He doesn't let you know that he's a movie star. He's just plain George. He's such a nice person, and everybody seems to like George because he reaches out to people."[18]

The premiere was the biggest thing to hit town probably since his aunt's movie opened in 1953. Indeed, the *Cincinnati Enquirer* quoted the historical coverage of that earlier premiere from the *Louisville Courier-Journal* and noted the similarities: "The picturesque old Ohio River town took on a carnival air. Streets were freshly washed down and manicured for the occasion. Lights and flags were strung across streets. Stores offered 'Rosemary Clooney Day' bargains. Every business and house had a 'welcome home' sign in the window."[19]

And so it was 55 years later, as planters were filled with new flowers to celebrate spring and the arrival of Clooney, Renee Zellweger, and *Leatherheads* in their town.

"It's just been an absolute madhouse," Maysville mayor David Cartmell said. "I did a [radio] show in L.A. They're all about George. We are too, baby. This is the Clooney tsunami."

Though tickets to the premiere at the 300-seat theater were in heavy demand, 16 were set aside for high school seniors from Mason County, St. Patrick, Augusta, and Bracken County high schools "so they could share their experience with future generations," Cartmell said. The rest were split among the Clooney family, government officials, and Washington Opera House donors.[20]

Hours before the comedy that Clooney directed, produced, and starred in rolled, the stars arrived on the red carpet in front of the Opera House. Authorities estimated the crowd at 2,000 people. Videos show people yelling at George, who stopped often along the ropes set up on Second Street to sign autographs, pose for pictures, and greet fans and friends. He can be heard on one video acknowledging a *Cincinnati Enquirer* reporter who had covered him for 20 years.

"I better do this for John Kiesewetter or he'll hit me—he'll hurt me—John!" Clooney joked.[21]

Kiesewetter was inside the Opera House when Cartmell honored the actors before the screening by declaring Monday Renee Zellweger Day in Maysville.

"And we proclaim every day in Maysville, Kentucky, to be George Clooney Day," Cartmell said.[22]

Clooney addressed the crowd, talking about why he had brought *Leatherheads* to Maysville.

"We've had marriages, wedding and funerals here . . . for 100 years. This is home for us," Clooney said. "This is something I've wanted to do for a long time. We're very proud to bring it full circle. As Rosemary said 55 years ago, it's nice to be home again."[23]

The story could end well here, where it began. But, though Clooney was still a Kentucky boy at heart, he undoubtedly belonged to the world, as evidenced yet again by his inclusion in *Time*'s May 2008 edition featuring what the magazine considered the 100 most influential people. Clooney was listed in the "Artists and Entertainers" section, and the article on him was written by his onetime boss, Roseanne Barr.

Her account of him is as spot-on as any, particularly in just over 200 words: "He breathes believability into his roles because he's real where it's hardest for actors to be: in life. Somehow he manages to be cool, handsome, and a standout while keeping that regular-guy thing going. He never looks like a pretty boy or a playboy, even though that is what he is by all tested and accepted movie-star standards. How can you not like—or at least not resent—someone who uses his fame to harangue the world (and what passes for its leaders) about the responsibilities of a free press and the horrors of Darfur or even the closer-to-home and lesser agonies of the writers' strike?"

Barr concluded, "I knew that George, 46, would be a big star years before you did. It was a great pleasure for the cast and crew of *Roseanne* to watch how he would craftily deliver lines, making them funny and sexy no matter how they read on the written page. He's a crack-up and a damn good sport. A favorite snack-table gossip-talk meet would start with 'Did you hear what Clooney did/said?' He can drink too much and still, while standing in a bar parking lot at 3 A.M., discuss the world with such passion and good sense that you actually stop imagining him nude and really listen."[24]

Meanwhile, someone who presumably had seen him nude quit listening. In June, the news hit the press that Clooney and girlfriend Sarah Larson had split up.[25] Just as after his breakup with Balitran, friends said he was doing fine. On a May weekend in Puerto Vallarta with the guys, an observer said, "he was smiling and seemed to be having a great time."[26]

Clooney's next film, *Burn after Reading*, was written by Joel and Ethan Coen, with whom Clooney had worked on O *Brother, Where Art Thou?*, and costarred Tilda Swinton, Clooney's *Michael Clayton* costar, as well as Clooney buddy and *Ocean's* costar Brad Pitt. Yes, the dark comedy about CIA secrets was a Clooney "family" affair, but not big at the box office after it opened, in September 2008.

Meanwhile, Clooney's Smoke House Productions was developing a half-hour comedy, *The Fall of Bob*, for Showtime. The series focused on a man narrating his life through flashbacks after jumping off a building, according to *Variety*. The company was also developing a TNT drama, *Delta Blues*.

For a while, Clooney seemed to fade from the spotlight. Most likely, however, during late 2008 he was busy working behind the scenes in support of Barack Obama's campaign for president. Knowing that a connection to the liberal George Clooney could hurt Obama, Clooney stayed away publicly but privately kept in touch. At one point, Clooney—ever the historical film buff, like his dad—suggested that Obama watch *The Candidate*, a 1972 Oscar-winning film starring Robert Redford as a character who might seem familiar to Obama: a charismatic liberal underdog running for the U.S. Senate.[27]

Clooney also found time to revisit Chad, this time with Pulitzer-prize winning journalist Nicholas Kristof of the *New York Times* (whose work had sparked Clooney's interest in the first place years earlier) and NBC's Ann Curry. Kristof's stories often began with anecdotes about Clooney, a tease to encourage the more celebrity-minded to pay attention to the horrors of Darfur.

"I was going to begin this column with a 13-year-old Chadian boy crippled by a bullet in his left knee, but my hunch is that you might be more interested in hearing about another person on the river bank beside the boy: George Clooney," one column began.

"Mr. Clooney flew in with me to the little town of Dogdoré, along the border with Darfur, Sudan, to see how the region is faring six years after the Darfur genocide began. Mr. Clooney figured that since cameras follow him everywhere, he might as well redirect some of that spotlight to people who need it more.

"It didn't work perfectly: No paparazzi showed up. But, hey, it has kept you reading at least this far into yet another hand-wringing column about Darfur, hasn't it?

"So I'll tell you what. You read my columns about Darfur from this trip, and I'll give you the scoop on every one of Mr. Clooney's wild romances and motorcycle accidents in this remote nook of Africa. You'll read it here way before *The National Enquirer* has it, but only if you wade through paragraphs of genocide."[28]

A couple of days later:

"So I'm bunking with George Clooney in a little room in a guest house here in eastern Chad, near Darfur in Sudan. We each have a mattress on the floor, the 'shower' is a rubber hose that doesn't actually produce any water, and George's side of the room has a big splotch of something that sure looks like blood.

"He's using me to learn more about Darfur, and I'm using him to ease you into a column about genocide. Manipulation all around—and, luckily, neither of us snores. (But stay tuned to this series for salacious gossip if he talks in his sleep.)"[29]

The lightheartedness dimmed a bit the next day, when there was some controversy about whether the United Nations had "pulled" Clooney's security, concerned that he, taking the trip as a private citizen and not as a Messenger of Peace, would criticize officials there.

Asked about the mini-controversy just a couple of days later, Clooney, always the one to downplay attention, sloughed it off. "I was never in jeopardy. I was with journalists who wanted to go into some areas that weren't particularly safe. And we decided that we would go. And that wasn't necessarily part of what the U.N. was looking to do. And so we just went on our own. It was fine," he said.[30]

Clooney's return from Chad coincided with the Academy Awards. His absence from the ceremony was notable, but the reason became obvious the next day, when he met with President Barack Obama and Vice-President Joe Biden to discuss his trip. Clooney was told that Darfur was one of a small number of areas being reviewed by high-level State Department officials. Afterward, Clooney announced to reporters that Obama would be appointing a full-time, high-level envoy to the region to report directly to the White House.[31]

An official statement from the vice president's office described the meeting.

"The Vice President met this evening with George Clooney to discuss Mr. Clooney's recent trip to Eastern Chad, where he visited Darfurian refugee camps," the statement read. "The Vice President informed Mr. Clooney about the Administration's ongoing review of Sudan policy and welcomed his observations from his trip. The Vice President thanked Mr. Clooney for his work on this issue, which he believes is an important contribution to the public's understanding of the conflict in Darfur."

In a move consistent with Clooney's popular movie/topical movie pattern and his goofball buddy/serious activist personality, the next news about Clooney was confirmation that he'd be providing the voice of Mr. Fox in an animated feature film, The Fantastic Mr. Fox. So, the man who swore kids weren't in his future continued to indulge the kid inside of him and to try new ways of diversifying his career.

And, for a brief moment in time in March 2009, 15 years after he began playing Dr. Doug Ross on NBC's ER, he returned to the series. For one unhyped night, Clooney was again Doug Ross to Juliana Margulies's Carol Hathaway. In one of the series wrap-up episodes that brought back departed cast members, Doug and Carol are working in a Seattle hospital transplant center where they convince the mother of a brain-dead boy to donate his organs. Two of the organs go to County General Hospital in Chicago, but Doug and Carol are never told that the kidney has been given to their old friend John Carter (Noah Wyle).

Rumors of Clooney's return had swirled for weeks, and leaks made it all but clear that, on March 12, Clooney would appear on the show, but it was uncertain whether the part would be just a cameo. The major portion of the episode featuring the popular Doug Ross kept the online community buzzing for days, and a ratings spike of 11 percent over the previous week accompanied his appearance.

A few weeks later, as the press was filled with the "end of an era" stories of *ER*'s last episode, which aired April 2, Clooney was in St. Louis filming *Up in the Air*. Locals were thrilled that Clooney would be in town nearly a month, and all confirmed to reporters that their encounters with him had proved that he was as "down to earth" and "un-Hollywood" as they come.[32]

So it ends as it began, with Clooney's reputation still solidly in the "nice guy" category. But life was moving on. His TV home, *ER*, was ending. The man who created that show, Michael Crichton, had died, on November 5, 2008. The man whose life Clooney had long sought to emulate also died, on September 27, 2008.

Whether Clooney will reach his goal to be endure in Hollywood and live his life like Paul Newman ("he set the bar too high for the rest of us," Clooney said) is anybody's guess. At least one Clooney fan believes he will.

"George is such a confident director, and he has no idea," said his friend and *Leatherheads* co-star, Renee Zellweger, nearly a year before Newman's death. "And he's a nice person. It gets boring hearing that, but it's true. Every once in a while you get the real good guy. You've got your Jimmy Stewart. You've got your Paul Newman. Now you've got your George Clooney."[33]

NOTES

1. "Clooney: Keep the Change, Kids," *Cincinnati Post*, April 5, 2007, p. C6.

2. "Warning! Celebs behind the Wheel," *Cincinnati Post*, September 22, 2007, p. D6.

3. Nick Clooney, "Catching up with the Clooneys," *Cincinnati Post*, September 28, 2007, p. B1.

4. David Germain, "Clooney Has it His Way as Actor, Filmmaker," *Cincinnati Post*, October 11, 2007, p. B1.

5. Ibid.

6. Ibid.

7. Ibid.

8. Ibid.

9. Ibid.

10. See http://www.people.com/people/article/0,,20180177,00.html.

11. All of the ceremony information is from a video of the Oscars. For video see http://www.youtube.com/watch?v=sr-zmHZWapY&feature=player_embedded; for transcript see http://www.mahalo.com/tilda-swinton-oscar-acceptance-speech.

12. Joel Stein, "Guess Who Came to Dinner?" *Time*, March 3, 2008, p. 46.

13. John Kiesewetter, "Fun in the Mud, with George and Renee," *Cincinnati Enquirer*, March 30, 2008, p. 1D.

14. Ian Parker, "Somebody Has to Be in Control," *New Yorker*, April 14, 2008, p. 40.

15. See http://www.youtube.com/watch?v=-QV85i5KaDg&feature=related.

16. Parker, "Somebody Has to Be in Control."

17. Ezra Buzzington, phone interview with author, March 21, 2008.

18. Gary Landers and Kevin Kelly, "Maysville Rolls Out the Red Carpet: Town Gets All Spiffed up for a 'Clooney Tsunami,'" *Cincinnati Enquirer*, March 22, 2008, p. A1.

19. Landers and Kelly, "Maysville Rolls Out the Red Carpet."

20. Ibid.

21. See http://www.youtube.com/watch?v=tvyox0OqUT8.

22. John Kiesewetter, "Maysville," *Cincinnati Enquirer*, March 25, 2008, p. 1A.

23. Ibid.

24. "Time 100," *Time*, May 12, 2008, p. 108.

25. Alexis Chiu with Mark Gray, "Calling it Quits," *People*, June 16, 2008, p. 70.

26. Ibid.

27. Kevin West, "G&R: After a Decade of Friendship: And Endless Romance Rumors—George Clooney and Renee Zellweger Are Costars at Last," *W.*, December 2007, p. 302.

28. Nicholas Kristof, "Trailing George Clooney," *New York Times*, February 19, 2009, p. A27.

29. Nicholas Kristof, "Sisters, Victims, Heroes," *New York Times*, February 22, 2009, p. 12.

30. Transcript of *Larry King Live*, CNN, February 23, 2009.

31. Amy Argetsinger and Roxanne Roberts, "A Chorus Calls for Song Rights," *Washington Post*, February 25, 2009, p. C3.

32. KPLR-TV St. Louis, news broadcasts April 1 and 2, 2009, www.cw11tv.com/pages/entertainment.

33. West, "G&R: After a Decade Of Friendship."

SELECTED BIBLIOGRAPHY

ARTICLES

Kennedy, Dana. "George Clooney and His Stormy Career." *New York Times*, June 25, 2000.

Kiesewetter, John, and Margaret A. McGurk. "Curious, Funny George." *Cincinnati Enquirer*, March 5, 2006.

Larsen, Dave. "George Clooney Shoots His Mouth Off." *Dayton Daily News*, June 28, 1998.

Lynch, Lorrie. "Why George Clooney Says: 'I Live for the Moment.'" *USA Weekend*, September 26–28, 1997.

O'Neill, Anne-Marie. "Boy George—At 40, George Clooney Seems as Committed as Ever to His Buddies, Basketball, a Certain Potbellied Pig—and Bachelorhood." *People*, May 7, 2001, 96.

Parker, Ian. "Somebody Has to Be in Control—The Effort behind George Clooney's Effortless Charm." *The New Yorker*, April 14, 2008.

Pearlman, Cindy. "Dr. Feelgood—Clooney Is Ready for Film Success." *Chicago Sun-Times*, June 21, 1998.

Rader, Dotson. "It's Finally about Friendship and Loyalty." *Parade*, June 7, 1998.

Riley, Jenelle. "Charismatic, Clooney Relies on More Than That." *Ventura County Star*, December 9, 2005.

Sanz, Cynthia. "The Sexiest Man Alive 1997/George Clooney." *People*, November 17, 1997.

Stein, Joel. "Guess Who Came to Dinner?" *Time*, March 3, 2008.

Stein, Joel. "The Wiz of Show Biz—George Clooney Knows You Think He's Slick and Pampered—and He'll Make You Like Him for It." *Time*, December 6, 2004.

BOOKS

Clooney, Nina. "George Clooney." In *Encyclopedia of Northern Kentucky*, ed. Paul A. Tenkotte. Lexington: University of Kentucky Press, 2009.

Cushman, Shana. *George Clooney, an Illustrated Biography*. London: Carlton Books, 2008.

Dougan, Andy. *The Biography of George Clooney*. Philadelphia: TransAtlantic, 1997.

Potts, Kimberly. *George Clooney—The Last Great Movie Star*. New York: Applause Theater & Cinema Books, 2007.

WEB SITES

Clooney Unlimited: www.clooneyunlimited.com

George Clooney Fan Site: www.gclooney.com

People: www.people.com/people/george_clooney

INDEX

Academy Awards, 25, 124–27, 142, 144, 151
Adler, Matt, 63, 73
Augusta, Kentucky, 5, 7–10, 16, 25, 26, 37, 64, 75, 89, 98, 108, 145, 147
Augusta High School, 9, 26, 31

Baby Talk, 47–49, 51
Balitran, Celine, 81, 98, 106, 149
Balsam, Talia, 46, 51
Barr, Roseanne, 45, 148–49
Batman & Robin, 35, 36, 63, 72, 74–77, 79, 105, 108, 117, 142, 145
Birnback, Nick, 137
Blessed Sacrament School, 3
Bodies of Evidence, 50, 51, 93
"The Boys," 37
The Building, 51
Burn After Reading, 143, 149
Buzzington, Ezra, 146–47

Cartmell, David, 147–48
Chicago Hope, 60, 61, 62

Crichton, Michael, 60, 63, 152
Clooney, Ada, 2, 3, 7, 18, 24, 26, 27
Clooney, Betty, 14, 22, 23, 24
Clooney, Nick, 1, 2, 4, 5, 8, 14–21, 23, 26, 33, 35, 36, 39, 45, 59, 101, 110, 112, 113, 116, 117, 125, 133, 134, 135; column 7, 9, 10, 21, 22, 60, 61, 62, 64, 69, 74, 88, 89, 90, 91, 98, 99, 117, 142
Clooney, Nina Warren, 2, 3, 4, 6, 7, 8, 16, 25–26, 31, 33, 69, 74, 88, 98, 116, 124, 136
Clooney, Rosemary, 1, 2, 3, 13, 14–15, 18, 22, 23–25, 37, 40, 46, 47, 59, 60–62, 65, 79, 109, 143, 145, 147, 148
Combat High, 45
Confessions of a Dangerous Mind, 110, 111

Darfur, 20, 133–37, 148, 150, 151
Delta Blues, 149
Denehy, Perry, 5, 7
Duffy, Julia, 49

Ebert, Roger, 73, 74, 79, 106, 127
ER, 14, 44, 52, 53, 57–64, 70, 71, 72, 74,
    81, 82, 85–88, 91, 93, 151–52
E/R, 38, 39, 40, 43

The Facts of Life, 40, 43, 44, 45
Fail-Safe, 89, 91–93
The Fall of Bob, 149
The Fantastic Mr. Fox, 151
Ferrer, Jose, 23, 33, 38, 39
Ferrer, Miguel, 33, 35, 50, 60
French, Heather, 8, 9–10, 25, 26, 27
From Dusk till Dawn, 62, 69, 71

Gaghan, Stephen, 119
Gilroy, Tony, 109, 143
The Good German, 142, 144
Good Night, and Good Luck, 115,
    117–21, 124, 126, 130, 144, 146
The Green Hornet, 71
Guilfoyle, George, 13, 14, 21–23,
    47, 49

Hard Copy, 98–100
Harpen, Anne, 3, 32
Harpen, Pete, 3, 5, 3
Heslov, Grant, 37, 40, 115, 121,
    124, 145
Hunt, Bonnie, 51, 57

Intolerable Cruelty, 111

A Journey to Darfur, 20, 134

Kiesewetter, John, 33, 43, 44, 49, 57, 58,
    62, 86, 92, 97, 148,
Kidman, Nicole, 76
Kidney Foundation of Greater Cincinnati,
    18, 64–65, 97
Kilroy, 89, 112
Kind, Richard, 37
Knights of the Kitchen Table, 49
Kramer, Kathy Penno, 34–35, 58
Kristof, Nicholas, 133, 150
K Street, 119

Larson, Sarah, 142, 144, 149
Lawrence, Bill, 35–36
Leatherheads, 81, 132, 141, 143, 145,
    147, 148, 152
Lopez, Jennifer, 77–80

Margulies, Juliana, 62, 151
Mathews, Thom, 37, 40
Max the pig, 45, 46, 57
Maysville, Kentucky, 8, 10, 14, 15, 17,
    22–26, 69, 145, 147–48
Maysville Pictures, 89
McAdam, Heather, 51–53
McAlpin's, 32, 35, 36, 37
Michael Clayton, 142–45, 149
Moonves, Les, 53, 58, 59, 92–93
Most Beautiful People, 63, 81, 93
Murrow, Edward R., 14, 15, 18, 21, 89,
    98, 115–17
Murrow and Me, 89, 93, 115

Newman, Paul, 78, 110, 152
Not On Our Watch, 135

Obama, Barack, 149, 151
Ocean's Eleven, 107, 111, 117, 143
Ocean's 12, 111
One Fine Day, 71, 72, 73, 76, 79
100 Most Influential People, 148
O'Reilly, Bill, 130–131
Oscar, 69, 119, 123, 124, 125, 126, 127,
    142, 144, 145, 149
Out of Sight, 77–79, 108, 109

The Peacemaker, 71, 72, 75, 76, 79, 91
The Perfect Storm, 91, 93, 105, 106
Pfeiffer, Michelle, 71, 73, 79
Pitt, Brad, 82, 135, 143, 149
The Predator, 37
Pressman, David, 133, 135
Preston, Kelly, 46

Rauch, Carol, 3
Red Surf, 47
Return of the Killer Tomatoes, 45, 70

Return to Horror High, 45
Riptide, 38
Rodriguez, Robert, 70, 71, 106
Roseanne, 45, 86, 149
Rosenfield, Stan, 62, 103, 111
Russell Theater, 14, 23

St. Michael's School, 3
St. Susanna Parish School, 3, 5, 6, 8
Schwartz, Virginia, 32, 37
Section Eight, 108, 109, 112, 120
Sellecca, Connie, 48, 49
Sexiest Man Alive, 76, 120, 126, 134
Shufeldt, John, 90
Sisters, 43, 51–53, 58, 59, 72, 93
Snowden, Lisa, 111, 112
Soderbergh, Steven, 78, 80, 81, 108–9,
    111, 120, 142
Solaris, 109, 142, 144
Spielberg, Steven, 63, 71, 75, 99
Spy Kids, 106
Stalkerazzi, 97–99
Stein, Joel, 145
Strathairn, David, 116
Street Hawk, 38
Sunset Beat, 46, 47, 51
Swinton, Tilda, 143, 145, 149

Syriana, 111, 112, 119–20, 123, 124–26,
    144, 145, 146

Tanner, Mary Ellen, 4, 24
The Thin Red Line, 81
Three Kings, 89–91,105, 106, 109, 119

United Nations, 129, 133, 135–38,
    150–51
Unscripted, 112, 119

Vicious, 38, 46

Walters, Barbara, 73, 125
Ward, Sela, 51, 53, 59–60
Warner Brothers, 58, 59, 64, 72, 90, 93
Warren, Dica, 65, 109
Weinberger, Ed, 48–49
Weintraub, Jerry, 135
Weiss, Ben, 37, 63
Wells, John, 57, 58, 59, 61, 87
Wesseler, Barb, 5–7
Western Row Elementary, 3, 5
Wyle, Noah, 71, 92, 152

Zellweger, Renee, 111, 142, 146, 147,
    148, 152

About the Author

JONI HIRSCH BLACKMAN is a columnist who has written her "Cul-de-sacs" newspaper column for 12 years in Naperville, Illinois. She is a former *People* magazine and *Time* magazine stringer and the author of hundreds of articles and columns for magazines such as *Family Life*, *Parenting*, *USA Weekend*, *Sports Illustrated for Kids*, and *Child*. Earlier in her career, she was a City Hall and education reporter for the *Denver Post*, a broadcast desk staffer for the Associated Press in Denver, and a feature writer for the *Brazosport Facts* in Clute, Texas. She began her career as a reporter for the *Arizona Daily Wildcat* in Tucson, Arizona. She was graduated from the University of Arizona, cum laude, with a B.A. in journalism.